WATERMELON
SNOW

LYNNE QUARMBY

WATERMELON SNOW

SCIENCE, ART,

and a LONE

POLAR BEAR

McGill-Queen's University Press
Montreal & Kingston • London • Chicago

ISBN 978-0-2280-0359-5 (cloth)
ISBN 978-0-2280-0508-7 (ePDF)
ISBN 978-0-2280-0509-4 (ePUB)

Legal deposit fourth quarter 2020
Bibliothèque nationale du Québec
Printed in Canada on acid-free paper that is 100% ancient forest free (100% post-consumer recycled), processed chlorine free

This book has been published with the help of a grant from the Simon Fraser University Publication Fund.

Funded by the Government of Canada · Financé par le gouvernement du Canada

Canada

Canada Council for the Arts · Conseil des arts du Canada

We acknowledge the support of the Canada Council for the Arts.
Nous remercions le Conseil des arts du Canada de son soutien.

Library and Archives Canada Cataloguing in Publication

Title: Watermelon snow : science, art, and a lone polar bear / Lynne Quarmby.
Names: Quarmby, Lynne, 1958- author.
Description: Includes bibliographical references and index.
Identifiers: Canadiana (print) 20200275720 | Canadiana (ebook) 20200275925 | ISBN 9780228003595 (cloth) | ISBN 9780228005087 (ePDF) | ISBN 9780228005094 (ePUB)
Subjects: LCSH: Quarmby, Lynne, 1958-—Travel—Norway—Svalbard. | LCSH: Climatic changes—Norway—Svalbard. | LCSH: Svalbard (Norway)—Description and travel.
Classification: LCC G780 .Q37 2020 | DDC 919.8/104512—dc23

The Uses of Sorrow

(In my sleep I dreamed this poem)

Someone I loved once gave me
a box full of darkness.

It took me years to understand
that this, too, was a gift.

– Mary Oliver

Contents

ix / Map of the High Arctic

x / Map of the Northwest Coast of Svalbard

3 / Watermelon Snow

173 / Acknowledgments

175 / Glossary and Notes

183 / Sources and Further Reading

187 / List of Crew and Participants

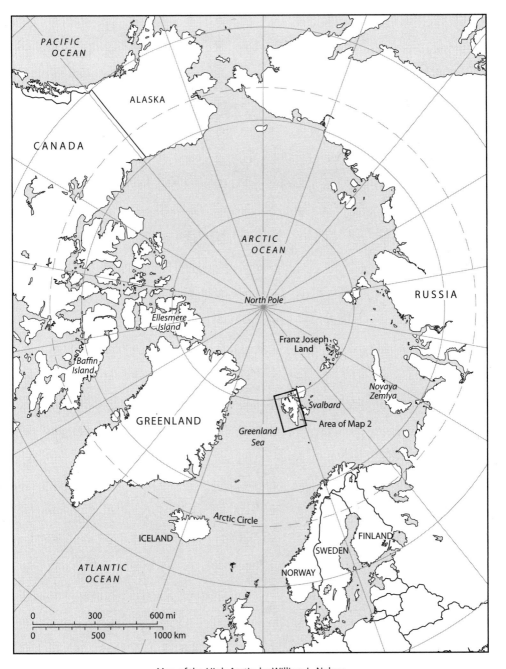

Map of the High Arctic, by William L. Nelson.

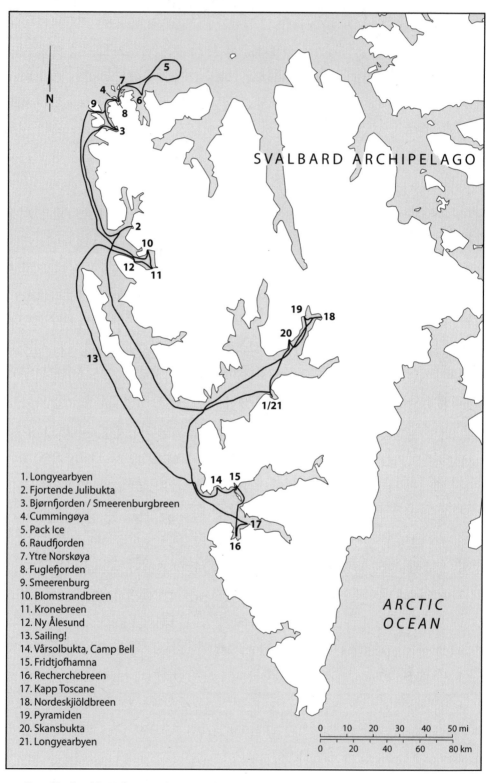

N

SVALBARD ARCHIPELAGO

5

7
4
6
9
8
3

2

10

12
11

19
18

20

13

1/21

14 15

17

16

1. Longyearbyen
2. Fjortende Julibukta
3. Bjørnfjorden / Smeerenburgbreen
4. Cummingøya
5. Pack Ice
6. Raudfjorden
7. Ytre Norskøya
8. Fuglefjorden
9. Smeerenburg
10. Blomstrandbreen
11. Kronebreen
12. Ny Ålesund
13. Sailing!
14. Vårsolbukta, Camp Bell
15. Fridtjofhamna
16. Recherchebreen
17. Kapp Toscane
18. Nordeskjiöldbreen
19. Pyramiden
20. Skansbukta
21. Longyearbyen

ARCTIC
OCEAN

0   10   20   30   40   50 mi
0   20   40   60   80 km

Map of Svalbard, by William L. Nelson. Coordinates for *Antigua*'s route provided by Sarah Gerats.

WATERMELON SNOW

There is nothing but ice, sea, and sky, whatever direction I look. I walk the perimeter of the floe – never closer than a metre from the edge, as much as I long to peer straight down. The air is still, the water calm and clear. An adjacent ice floe plunges several metres below the surface in diminishing turquoise contours. Above the water, the ice edge glows lapis blue, reflecting like a glaze on the turquoise below. Nearby, a pair of eiders swims along an ice edge. Above the ice, horizontal clouds line up in a dozen soft, thin rows, subtle swaths of grey, pink, and dusty purple, the colour of a fresh-picked plum before you polish it for eating. My eyes fill with tears.

After years of fighting for political action on global warming – civil disobedience, lawsuits, a run for Parliament – hearing about, reading about, and seeing various graphs of melting summer sea ice, here I stand on an actual sheet of melting summer sea ice, bearing witness. It's emblematic of our warming world; it's an abstraction – and yet also cold, hard, blue, real. I quietly weep. I see the melting away of democracy and the melting of the ice and I know these are tightly entwined. Joining many others, I poured my soul into the work. We have barely made a dent in altering the course of "business as usual."

Out here on the floe edge, I am struggling with burnout and despair. I am travelling on a schooner, a scientist on an artists' residency. The voyage – and the book it conjured – is a search for rational, meaningful responses to the global environmental crisis, a search for life beyond despair.

EXPEDITION

In the remote international territory of the Svalbard archipelago, land of glaciers and polar bears, halfway between Norway and the North Pole, twenty-eight artists and two scientists (including me) are making final preparations for an expeditionary residency. Over the past week, we've been arriving by plane in Longyearbyen, a coal-fired town (population 2,000) on the shore of a protected bay in the large fjord, Isfjorden. It's Sunday, 10 June 2017. A few of us arrived near midnight last night and were shuttled by bus to our accommodation in the Coal Miners' Cabins, about two and a half kilometres up the valley. A glacier, hanging from a mountain high above the cabins, glistened in the sunshine. This afternoon, I am in the Coal Miners' Bar & Grill, where a row of windows looks out on a rock-strewn meadow patched with snow and last year's brown grass. I finish assembling my microscope and stand to watch as an Arctic fox runs by, wearing a mottled transitional coat, part winter, part summer. I feel the barest hint of awe. Mostly, I feel irritable. I'm having a hard time making conversation and I am annoyed with myself for being out of sorts when I am finally here, in the high Arctic.

My return flights from Vancouver to Longyearbyen will put almost four tonnes of carbon into the atmosphere, more than the weight of eight adult polar bears or one baby blue whale, effectively doubling my annual carbon footprint. Am I fooling myself to think there is anything I can do to make this up to the bears, the whales, or my son?

I emerge into the overcast day. There is not much choice about where to go. Here at the top of the valley, we are at the end of the road.

The mountain rises steeply beyond the road and behind the cabin; on the other side of the road are a few buildings, beyond which the valley opens up for perhaps two hundred metres in a rough meadow of rocks and mud, snow and water. In any of these directions, there is nothing but wilderness between me and the next polar bear. We've been sternly warned not to venture off on our own without an armed guide. I start down the road toward town and the beach.

Just ahead are Carleen, an American visual artist about my age (late fifties); Pablo, almost middle-aged, currently of Copenhagen, here to explore what he calls "pioneerism"; and Adam, a bearded British cine-matographer of sublime landscapes. I join them, and the four of us walk down the valley together. In the distance, beyond the drab buildings of town, the deep indigo of the fjord carries my eye to snow-patched mountains on the other side. I am glad of the company, but I don't participate in the conversation; I focus on photographing the mud and rivulets, and the occasional pink-footed goose.

On the side of the mountain, below the broken timbers and black smudge of an abandoned coal mine, a reindeer grazes on moss and lichens. We arrive in town, stopping to wonder at two badly damaged houses, contorted and sitting at strange angles. These must be two of the eleven houses destroyed by the 2015 avalanche. Twenty people were trapped in the houses and nine buried by snow. The avalanche happened during a severe winter storm, yet the community managed an impressive rescue effort that limited fatalities to two people. I look at the slopes of the mountains on either side of the valley. It seems like a strange place to build a town, but then, this is where the coal was found. And it is a beautiful setting.

We find our way to the group gathering on the beach for the welcome party, organized by Sarah, our lead guide. Sarah is in her mid-thirties, and with her Arctic blue eyes, matching blue down sweater, and short, blonde hair tucked under a blue wool headband, she looks of this place. She is attractive, and enigmatic in the way of those who say little. When Sarah arrived in Svalbard "by accident" seven years ago, it was as a performance artist. She became a local, learning how to use bear bangers and shoot a rifle. Now she is a wilderness guide, and on our trip, Sarah will be the expedition leader.

Tims, one of the other guides, lights a bonfire that draws in those who have been wandering the beach. There are no boats on the calm water.

A pair of eiders flies low over the reflective surface. We stand around the fire, or sit on shipping pallets and improvised benches. A man arrives, his arms full with a bundle of reindeer pelts. He and a few others, I later learn, are locals, Sarah's friends, but at this point I am uncertain about who's who. I watch some from our group inspect the pelts. Pablo lifts one from an end and I can see it is stiff like a piece of cardboard. These are country pelts – hunted and tanned. These are pelts for sitting on at a beach party in Longyearbyen.

Sarah returns carrying a large pot of something hot, prepared in her small wooden house, just a few yards away. With her is Emma, her arms full of bread and bowls. Emma is Australian, one of Sarah's friends from the world of performance art. She moves like a dancer and is relaxed, greeting people like old friends. Some *are* old friends; Emma has been here before. She is here this time to participate as an artist on the expedition. I hang back for a bit and then help myself to a bowl of chickpea curry from the steaming kettle. It tastes like the best chickpea curry ever, and I smile because I know I will try, but this taste will never be replicated in my kitchen at home. In the city, there are no substitutes for the seasonings of fresh sea air, mountain vistas, and time spent walking close to the wild.

I feel strangely shy. After thirty years of attending science conferences, this is my first artist residency. These aren't my people; this isn't my tribe. I'm curious and want to be friendly, but I can't seem to muster the energy to engage with new people. I hide behind my camera, watching the artists talking and laughing as if they've known one another for years. Some of them have. I overhear my roommate M catching up with Cara on personal news since the last residency they'd been on together. Risa and Robert are discussing the Canadian art scene, about which I know nothing.

The sun has come out from behind the clouds and the low angle of the light warms the indigo, rust, and mustard paint of the simple metal and wooden houses that follow the curve of the shore. The golden hour for photography – that time after sunrise and before sunset when the low angle of the sun provides a soft warm light – distorts into hours of magical light, here where the sun rises and dips but never drops below the horizon. Pools of flat water, left on the rocky beach by the ebbing tide, reflect mountains with every bowl, valley, and north face still carrying last season's snow.

I am curious to see inside Sarah's house, so I tag along when I overhear her offer the use of her washroom to one of the artists. Sarah's space is perhaps four hundred square feet, rustic and rough hewn, but entirely adequate. I fantasize about living here and I see the seasons flow by in my imagination. I shudder at the thought of winter's perpetual darkness.

We are about to make a fifteen-day journey aboard the tall ship, *Antigua*, exploring the western and northern coasts of Svalbard. There will be forty-two of us on the ship: the captain and his crew of first and second mate plus deckhand, the cook and his staff of three, four wilderness guides, thirty "participants," and one dog. This is the ninth year of the Arctic Circle Expeditionary Residency, which runs two trips a year to the edge of the Arctic sea ice. As we embark on the summer solstice trip, another group anticipates sailing in the shortening days and expansive night skies of autumn.

A goal of the program is to foster interdisciplinary engagement on current issues. The twenty-eight artists in our group include an architect, a marine biologist, a teacher, and others with interests in science and global issues. The two of us who were selected as scientists each have a foot in the art world and a record of advocacy or activism. It's an expensive trip and each of us pays our own way, many with the help of grants and sponsorships. This will be a working trip for all of us and I am here to find watermelon snow. During summer blooms, microscopic algae turn snowfields watermelon-red. They increase the rate of snowmelt and may be amplifying global warming.

Around midnight, under a sunny sky, we start leaving the beach in small groups for the walk back up the valley to our bunks in the Coal Miners' Cabins. Back in our room, I find M already in their bunk by the window, but still awake. The room is stifling and we don't seem to have a way to control the heat. Together we figure out the unusual latch on the window and open it wide, feeling safe from polar bears, here on the second floor. Safe from bears, perhaps, but not from the knowledge that a coal plant is generating the heat we are spilling out the open window.

Longyearbyen is a frontier town and its coal mining history is celebrated, not least with the statue of a miner in the town square. It's also home to the Svalbard Global Seed Vault, where over twenty million seeds – including 930,000 varieties of food crops from around the world – are stored in a vault in the permafrost, designed to preserve the seeds in the event of global catastrophe. We are unable to visit the Seed Vault because just two weeks before we arrived, the entrance tunnel flooded with gushing melt water after the warmest winter ever recorded. The vault itself was not breached, the seeds are safe, and the facility is undergoing "technical improvements." The irony of the flood is sharpened by knowing the Seed Vault opened in 2008, less than a decade ago. What does this tell us about preparing for a future that will be different from anything we've known?

After a few hours in bed, I give up on sleep, dress quietly, and leave M softly snoring. Downstairs, I put on my red parka and recently resoled hiking boots, and navigate through the mud and an impromptu stream, making my way a few metres uphill to the Coal Miners' Bar & Grill, hoping it's open and warm and filled with the smell of fresh-brewed coffee (it's 5 a.m.). The day is overcast and in spite of the beauty that I know surrounds us, there isn't much to look at besides patches of dirty snow and muddy streams. I listen to the sounds of running water.

The door to the Bar & Grill is open. In the anteroom, I take off my muddy boots and too-warm parka and mount the short flight of stairs to the bar in my stocking feet. I don't smell coffee. Sitting just inside the entrance I recognize Justin – thirty-something with a dirty blond beard and longish hair in the style of Einstein, the original bedhead. He is slouched in a big easy chair and barely stirs to say, "Hey." He looks miserable. "Yeah," he says. "I'm waiting for things to open so I can get something for this cold. I have a fever."

I offer to go back to my room to get him some ibuprofen from my first aid kit. Back in my parka and boots, I navigate the mud down to my room in the building that was once home to seventy-two coal miners. Already, I'm tiring of the tedium of the on-and-off with my heavy hiking boots every time I enter a building. I'm feeling grumpy from lack of sleep, resentful that both parka and boots are overkill in the warmth of a melting Arctic. I trudge back up the hill.

For now, Justin and I are the only patrons in the Bar & Grill. This time, I smell the aroma of coffee brewing. I settle in at a table with my laptop, getting ready to catch up on writing in my journal, relishing the thought of some quiet time for this headache to subside before the others arrive for breakfast. Suddenly, there is a retirement-age Norwegian man with a broad face sitting at my table (in this empty room!). "I'm travelling alone, but my English is very good," he says. I groan silently. Is he

hitting on me? Surely not. I'm a bit embarrassed at my thoughts, but ...
why is he at my table? I am not in the mood for conversation, and yet,
I am travelling and he is (more or less) a local. Because I don't want to be
rude, I listen. I learn he is from central Norway, and coming to Svalbard
has been a lifelong ("forty years at least") dream of his. He has been
here three days and goes home today. "I've been out on a boat. Saw some
whales." He talks about coal miners – there were miners in his family.
I suppose I'm encouraging him because soon he is exuberantly telling
me about yesterday's adventure: "I met some men from a choir and we
were friends for a day! Lots of drinking! Crazy stuff! I bought a woman
for one of the men! But it was only a joke!"

After breakfast with the Norwegian, I catch a ride down the valley to
UNIS – University Centre in Svalbard. I add my muddy boots to the rows
by the door and wander the empty halls of the university in my socks
until I find a technician from one of the biology labs. I'm looking for a
few millilitres of chemical fixative to preserve samples of cells to take
home – the fixative is common, but toxic, and I hadn't wanted to deal
with all of the paperwork of bringing some from my lab in Canada. The
technician finds a bottle of glutaraldehyde and pours a few millilitres into
a fifteen-millilitre screw top plastic tube I've brought for this purpose.
Also in my pocket is a bar of Lindt Sea Salt Dark Chocolate, carried from
Vancouver for this very transaction. Whenever I've been somewhere
remote, chocolate, coffee, and alcohol have been commodities of value
for bartering. I offer it to the technician and he looks puzzled. Then he
smiles and we both laugh at the unusual exchange. I hike back up the
valley to organize and pack my gear.

Early afternoon, we gather outside the Bar & Grill with our luggage
to await the bus that will take us to the ship. The piles of gear astound
me. I can't imagine what these impractical artists are bringing aboard.
I have my microscope in its case, a box of small equipment, a small duffle
bag of clothing, and a daypack of camera gear – a compact, if heavy, kit.
We stuff our gear into the compartments under the bus and board for
the ten-minute ride down the valley to Longyearbyen. We turn left on
the road that follows the shoreline out to Svalbard Airport, but we go
only so far as the docks.

I leave the bus and there at the dock is the tall ship *Antigua*. I feel
a surge of excitement. She is beautiful. Wooden decks and rails, a deep

indigo hull with a white stripe along the gunwales, an elegant bowsprit, three tall masts, and a seemingly excessive amount of rigging. The main deck is about eight feet below the fore and aft decks. On the aft deck sits the wheelhouse. Built in 1957 as a fishing boat, the *Antigua* was later refit in the style of a traditional tall-mast schooner – I have not yet realized that a good portion of our travelling will be propelled by a diesel engine and that we will only hoist the sails once, albeit for a run that will last almost twenty-four hours. Today, I simply wonder at her size. The *Antigua* is only fifty metres long and seven metres wide and looks too small for all of our gear and us. Still, I am happy that for the next fifteen days, this beautiful boat will be my home.

We wait patiently as the groceries that will feed us are loaded and stowed. A box of potatoes, a box of carrots, a box of onions, a case of dill pickles. Soon, it's time to load our gear. A loose and disorganized bucket brigade forms, falls apart after a few precious pieces are loaded under the close watch of their owner, and forms again as another artist supervises the loading of awkward packages. I marvel at the variety of sizes and shapes, and wonder what can be inside. By the time we are invited aboard, the pile of gear fills the main deck and it doesn't look like there is room for us. At last I walk across the gangplank from the dock to the aft deck, my heart dancing and my stomach tingling. At last!

It has been cloudy all day, but now the clouds break and I feel the warmth of sunshine on my face. We each grab what we can of our gear and file down the steep steps, almost a ladder, to our berths below the main deck. Most of us take two or more trips. The crew directs traffic as we struggle with large and heavy bags. In a surprisingly short time, the deck is clear and we begin to settle in.

M and I are in cabin number six, midship, starboard. M doesn't talk much and I am not much in the mood for talking. It is going to take a while for us to get to know one another. They want the bunk under the porthole and I am fine with the bunk closer to the centre of the ship – perhaps there will be a little less rocking motion here. Roommates were assigned before we left home and there was time to do a little research. I found a photo of one of M's works of art. It is an installation composed of lumber, caution tape, rope, cement blocks, and traffic cones. In the centre, two life-size lawn-ornament deer, spray-painted silver, with antlers that look like oak trees in winter, face off.

We are unpacking – organizing personal items on shelves and stowing gear under our bunks – when Cara knocks on our cabin door to pass along word that the captain is calling us up to the salon. The salon is at the aft of the ship, under the wheelhouse. It's a room of brass and polished wood, with a bar, a buffet area, three big tables, and a pleasing amount of natural light from several portholes and an overhead skylight. Captain Joachim Schiel – or Captain Joe, as he says to call him – is compact and fit, with an air of authority that tells us we're in good hands. He welcomes us aboard and introduces us to the crew, the chef, and the service team. Captain Joe lets us know how best to live respectfully aboard his ship. He gives detailed instructions about our boots (two pair each, gumboots and hiking boots), how to stow them neatly in pairs by the salon door, and how to wash the grit and salt from them after visiting shore. This involves swishing our feet in the sea before boarding the Zodiacs for the shuttle from shore to ship, and then a scrub and a rinse at the fresh water boot-washing station as we board the *Antigua*. We're taught the importance of signing on and off the ship. We learn we'll each be fitted with a numbered life jacket for all shore excursions, and to bring on deck with us should there be an emergency. Captain Joe warns us of the dangers of falling overboard into the icy Arctic waters. He concludes by asking us to take three-minute showers to conserve water. Then, we cast off.

After leaving the protected waters of Isfjorden we hit the rougher waters of the Greenland Sea on the west coast of Spitsbergen (the largest island of the archipelago) and turn north into the wind. There is a slight chop to the sea. The sky is a brilliant blue, interrupted by straps of mist so thick it seems here at the top of the world is where clouds are born. The mountains rise directly from the sea, but they are without trees. These are not alpine peaks rising sharply above the tree line; they are gentle, low-elevation mountains, whose vegetation is set by latitude, not altitude. Swaths of mountainside glow a beautiful, soft moss green in the late evening sun.

Spending a day in a frontier town allowed us to decompress from the intensity of "civilization." And now, after jetting to Longyearbyen from our far-flung homes, we are travelling at a pace befitting a journey into another world.

I need this time. I stand apart on the aft deck, a confusing swirl of emotion making it difficult to engage with my fellow travellers. I am overwhelmed. I've dreamed of the high Arctic since I was a little girl, and yet I've managed to arrive run down and irritable. I am annoyed with myself. It will take me another year to appreciate that I am dealing with something bigger than recovery from burnout – that I need to learn how to live with a grief I haven't yet had the courage to face.

A dozen years ago, I started reading about global warming and the climate crisis. I can't say now why it took me so long, other than life: a son, a divorce, research grants. But eventually, like a slap in the face, I saw the need for urgent action. I acted like the house was on fire. I joined others fighting for climate action and gave it everything I had. And now, the house is still on fire, but I am tired and irritable. I am angry at everyone. None of us is doing enough. Nothing is enough. Standing on the deck as we travel deeper into the mythic Arctic, I feel bereft.

When I look at the continuing year-over-year rise in carbon dioxide levels and see the staggering impact of our species ... the weight of it crushes me. I am overwhelmed and cannot process the human suffering caused by wildfires, famines, superstorms, floods, and heat waves. I mourn with a mother whale – one of the last members of the southern resident orca – who carried her dead calf for seventeen days. My body aches when I think of the loss of the old growth forests where I grew up on Vancouver Island. These rich forests are succumbing to the greed of excessive logging, an activity that further accelerates global warming. Causes. Effects. I protested pipelines and coal ports because I could not stand by and watch the construction of new infrastructure to support the continued – expanded! – use of fossil fuels. The protests delayed construction of the pipeline. But for how long?

Then, to the port side, the fog thins to reveal a quiet symphony of grey playing on the water – oyster, pearly, mousy, and leaden; in the distance, the mountains are a muted slate. Gone are the golden mossy slopes, replaced by a sublime seascape of white fog, silver water, and looming black mountains, a world completely other. The air is still. I am knocked out of my own misery, my own story. For a few moments I feel alone in the wilderness, serene and elated.

The crew sets anchor in the calm waters of Fjortende Julibukta. Some distance across the water a glacier emerges as the fog drifts. It looks as cold as a silver moon. How far are we from the glacier face? Without distance I can't begin to gauge size, and without size I've no idea how far.

Floating in front of the glacier are icebergs. Some of the floating ice emits an eerie sky-blue light – how can that be? That ethereal blue light can't be real! The inability to judge size and distance will stay with me throughout the trip, as will the feeling of otherworldliness.

ON PERCEPTIONS

It is impossible to constantly remember that everything we perceive with our senses, and our responses to those perceptions, has been honed by billions of years of natural selection. We rarely, if ever, pause to consider that what we are experiencing is a filtered and heavily biased version of the world, which we mistake for "reality."

If you fill a tiny glass tube with a sugar solution, and then hold the tip in a dish of water, the sugar will seep out into the dish, forming a gradient – lots of sugar near the mouth of the tube, less farther away. If there are bacteria in that dish of water, they will soon gather around the mouth of the tube. The bacteria will have sensed sugar in the dish and managed to navigate their way to its source. This is more of a miracle than it might seem at first glance. If you crunch the numbers, the bacterium couldn't possibly know which way to go.

The concentration of sugar is high near the mouth of the tube, and drops off farther from the source. It seems simple: the bacteria swim in the direction of increasing sugar concentration. Indeed, these tiny single-celled organisms can sense the sugar concentration. The surface of each bacterial cell is sprinkled with molecules that have a special shape that sugar snuggles into – for a short while. These molecules, called receptors, change shape when holding sugar, so the amount of time spent holding sugar versus being empty can be interpreted by the cell and used as an indicator of sugar concentration. So far, so good. But the bacteria are very tiny and the difference in sugar concentration from one side of the cell to the other is miniscule. To the *E. coli*, the concentration of sugar appears to be the same all around the cell. How can the cells possibly know which way to go to find the source of sugar?

E. coli use a system that is much like a drunk finding his way home; they use a "biased random walk." Imagine the jelly bean–shaped cell, festooned with ten long, helical flagella, all spinning. If they are spinning counterclockwise, the ten flagella twine together, forming a single propeller that drives the cell in a "run." But if the flagella spin clockwise, then they unwind, and the cell tumbles. After a tumble, the flagella spin counterclockwise, form a propeller, and the cell is off on another run – in a random new direction. Clockwise rotation – tumbling – is suppressed when surface receptors are bound to sugar. Suppressed tumbling in the presence of sugar means straight runs last longer.

If a run happens to take the cell further away from food, the cell surface receptor will spend more time empty (because the concentration of sugar is lower) and the cell will soon tumble to try another direction. In other words, the random walk is biased towards the direction of the sugar by altering the probability of clockwise rotation and tumbling. Our hypothetical drunk stumbles about until the sighting of a familiar landmark spurs a stretch of purposeful walking, which lasts until once again nothing is recognizable and the drunk stumbles off in a random new direction, eventually finding home. In the same way, the bacteria find their way to the sugar.

One last detail about *E. coli* swimming to sugar. Including the receptors, there are at least fifteen components in the *E. coli* sensory system that modulate the proclivity of the rotary motor for changing direction. Without a system for setting the gain, the cells would quickly lose the ability to detect a change in sugar concentration – too high or too low and the receptor would be occupied constantly or not at all.

Now, here is the truly remarkable thing: our human sensory systems use similar components in much the same way as *E. coli*. For example, the molecules that detect light hitting our eyes are strikingly similar to those *E. coli* uses to detect sugar. And the way our eyes adjust to the dark parallels how the *E. coli* system adjusts its sensitivity the closer it gets to the source of sugar. Both our vision and our olfaction use modified versions of the molecular components that *E. coli* uses to sense food and toxins in its environment.

What this means is that the molecular machinery for sensing the environment evolved during the emergence of life on Earth. Sensing the environment and responding appropriately to changes in that environment are fundamental to life. A necessity, not an accoutrement.

Yet, there is much about our environment we don't sense. Our ability to sense and respond to the environment is severely limited, both by the options presented by evolution and the importance of a particular sense or response to our survival.

Climate change is happening so fast it should be terrifying. It should feel like the time I was caught in a riptide, watching my young son on the shore as I was pulled out to sea. Or that sudden fear I felt one late afternoon in a gentle snowstorm, skiing out from a backcountry cabin, when out of the thick fog we came upon the same landmark for the second time in an hour. And yet I don't feel terror, even here. The Arctic may be ground zero for climate change, but it's difficult to directly experience that reality. Because of the knowledge I carry, I feel sadness and anger, but not terror. Occasionally, when I do feel fear, it is not the sudden, bowel-churning fear of being lost on a winter mountain, but rather an anxiety, a nervousness. My limited senses deny me direct experience of climate change. My delusions render terror impossible.

On this ship, I drift from railing to railing. Across the bay, thousands of birds are swooping and diving into the water. The glacier seems close, but I can't hear the birds and they look to be the size of mosquitoes. Suddenly, a cloud of them lifts from the floating ice where they had been invisibly resting; they burst into the sky like a small explosion. An instant later, we hear a loud crack followed by a crashing sound, and then a splash as a piece of the glacier cleaves off and falls into the sea. The glacier has calved a new iceberg. Happily warm in my parka, I watch as the waves generated by the birth approach. I don't hear the radio waves passing from the ship to the guides' walkie-talkies as they scout for a landing. I can't feel the concentration of carbon dioxide in the air, and, in spite of the calving, I can't tell whether on balance Fjortende Julibreen is advancing or retreating. My direct experience of the world is limited in time, in space, and by senses evolved to keep me (and my kin) alive.

In his 2017 book, *Why Buddhism Is True*, Robert Wright presents a convincing case that natural selection underlies the delusions that cause human suffering as described by the Buddha in his teachings on the Four Noble Truths. We haven't evolved to perceive reality as it is, but rather, natural selection has honed our perceptions of the world to be biased and distorted in whatever ways best serve our success at reproduction – a sure recipe for delusion. When we act in ways that are not aligned with reality, we cause suffering for ourselves and others. Mindfulness helps us see the world more clearly by recognizing the emotionality that colours our perceptions. Science (and technology) expands our ability to sense reality. From these clarified and expanded views, our delusions are exposed.

It's June in the high Arctic and there are twenty-four hours of daylight. Perhaps this, too, contributes to the disorientation that has opened me to a keener sense of the distinction between my perceptions and reality. On the evolutionary timescale, it has been the blink of an eye since Copernicus realized – and Galileo observed – that there is day and night because we live on a spinning world that orbits the Sun. We are still trying to get used to the idea. What we know to be reality is not always reflected in how we experience the world, as A. R. Ammons illustrates in this short poem:

Spaceship

It's amazing all
this motion going
on and
water can lie still
in glasses and the gas
can in the
garage doesn't rattle.
– A. R. Ammons

Our direct sensory experience of the world evolved with us; in our hearts the world is what our sensory organs tell us it is. Our senses are superbly effective for helping us function in the everyday world – that is why we are still here. So it's understandable that when science reveals something counterintuitive or paradoxical, we have difficulty integrating the new ideas into our worldview. Here in the Arctic, with a sun that doesn't set, it seems easier to recognize and acknowledge that my direct biological senses, as wonderful as they are, give me only a tightly pinched and cloudy view of the world. As the waves from the crashing iceberg arrive, I feel the undulation of the ship. I feel a cold breeze on my face. For a moment, I intuit a glimmer of the rich reality beyond my limited senses. In this astonishingly beautiful place, I feel open to unimagined beauty.

EXPEDITION

After our first breakfast on the *Antigua* – sliced meats, cheeses, and cucumber; fresh bread, preserves, and Nutella; medium-soft-boiled eggs; fresh fruit – we're shuttled by Zodiac to an expansive spit at the south end of the bay. The spit is perhaps fifty metres across. I stand on the high point and use my binoculars to scan snowy hills across the channel for hints of red or pink. I see only white snow and am mildly perplexed. Conversations with scientists who have collected snow algae here in Svalbard led me to expect that watermelon snow would be easy to find. But it's early in the expedition and early in the season – there is still time.

I look around at my shipmates, people I'm just getting to know, twenty-eight artists and Jessamyn, a physicist who uses stand-up comedy as her art, a way of communicating science and shaking up perceptions of women in science. After a night in the close quarters of the ship, the thirty of us casually spread out, maximizing inter-person distance – bounded by the sea and by a perimeter established by our guides, who stand watch, armed, and with eyes peeled for the approach of polar bears. Susan, a photographer and activist from Vancouver, crouches low, photographing lichen-covered rocks in the centre of the gravel spit, bright yellow, orange, and grey lichens. All around us are clumps of purple saxifrage in full bloom over their thin beds of dark green foliage, and brownish red and green succulents. They barely rise above the gravel, a composite of sand and pebbles. It's a delight to discover this small and beautiful life on land that looked desolate from the ship. I recall Captain Joe's request that we tread with care; things take decades to grow here.

In addition to studying snow algae, I'm here because I'm fascinated by art, even though I don't know much about it. Indeed, I often feel that I don't get it; I don't know how to read it. Sometimes, alone, late at night, I paint. I'm private about painting because I reject labels like "hobbyist" or "dabbler" – not because I'm any good, but because it means too much to me. I pour my soul into painting and I pester artist friends with wretched questions like, "What is art?" The differences between art and science seem radical and obvious; I'm interested in the similarities, the possibilities for exploration and discovery.

I'm keen to learn how the artists on this residency are approaching their work, given our moment. It is surreal to find myself a biologist at a unique time in the approximately four-billion-year history of life on Earth, when geological-scale changes are happening in the span of my own existence. What is in store? What will I live to see? While every generation has its moment, never in the entire existence of humanity has there been a time as singular as this one. Within the span of a human lifetime, there will be changes in climate and sea levels that will dwarf the oscillations between ice ages. No human has ever seen extinctions, climate chaos, and receding shorelines like those of us alive today are on track to witness. How are these artists responding?

After awkwardly walking the steep beach of loose pebbles on the exposed side of the spit, I return to the high point – about two metres above the tideline – where the ground is firm under my feet. I notice that many of the artists are working on the inland, glacier-facing side of the spit where the beach is sandy and the slope gentler. Emma is dancing. She's dressed all in white, in long pants, and a long-sleeved shirt. She flows through a routine that will become familiar – elegant high kicks, leaps, and graceful tumbles on the sand. As Emma explains to me later, she's exploring how we make the same mistakes over and over. Recently, on the deck of a freighter crossing the Atlantic from New York City to Rotterdam, Emma danced every day, the same choreography over and over. The white dress that she wore with its dirty marks from the deck will be exhibited beside this white suit, with the marks that will accumulate from dances at our landings.

With some help, an older British painter named Charles lugged his enormous sketchpad on and off the Zodiac and up the beach. It must be three feet by five feet, thick and heavy. Now he's sketching the distant glacier in big, bold brushstrokes. Cara, a sculptor and multimedia artist from LA, has her camera trained on Mylar balloons in the shapes of letters, bouncing in the breeze. Many of the artists are busy with their projects, but I notice I'm not the only one wandering around the spit, taking photos and just standing and staring, soaking up the place. I wonder if the other wanderers are feeling lost and overwhelmed, like me. I feel I should be doing something, but I don't know what.

This lack of direction is feeding my discomfort and irritability. I don't yet realize that this time with nothing to do is precisely what I need. I don't yet see that my constant pushing to get things done not only led to my burnout, but also kept me from recognizing that I was in denial.

We crowd together again aboard the ship for lunch, boisterous and friendly. There is much excited conversation about the scenery and the soup – a delicious aromatic vegetable soup in clear broth. I can hardly wait to get back outside and I am ready with my life jacket for the first shuttle to shore. The afternoon landing is on a narrow beach at the north end of the glacier.

The geography of this place is as disorienting as its scale. We've landed on a moraine beach backed by a wall of ice that runs perpendicular to the glacier face. The wall of ice is like an arm of the glacier, reaching out to embrace us. In fact, the ice wall is a remnant of the receding glacier, clinging to the mountain behind it. At first, it seems that we will be able to walk along the beach, along the arm of ice, all the way to the glacier. But soon, we run out of beach. We are blocked by a promontory of ice. Between the glacier and us remains a stretch of water. It looks a hundred metres wide, but I suspect it might be much more. Whatever the distance, we are not as close as I yearn to be.

Fjortende Julibreen towers in front of us, white, but blue, and cold. A few of us cluster near the end of the beach, frustrated that the service staff from the *Antigua* are taking a smoke break between us and the glacier. We don't know them yet, and it takes a few moments before we are laughing together at their nonchalance and our excitement. I capture the sought-after photograph: a gravel beach of shiny wet stones in the foreground, still water reflecting a subtle spectrum of colours from the ice and sky, the icy face of the glacier in blues and whites with misty clouds above. I am thrilled to capture a momentary parting of the clouds that reveals a dramatic mountain peak, craggy and rocky with snowy faces, looming above the glacier. There is some joking among the artists about us all capturing our "postcard shots." I'm intrigued to hear them playing with the question of whether pretty pictures are art. I wonder what distinguishes the sublime landscape images captured by artists like Adam and Hailey. Or the spectacular pieces Risa will make from this shot – an enormous and dramatic print on fabric, and a large needlework piece. I imagine each stitch as a snowflake contributing to the glacier, memorialized as it melts. The laughter subsides and we slowly and quietly spread out along the shore.

Above the tideline, the beach is a mess of mud and rock; below the tideline, where the mud has washed away, the beach is rocky with sandy patches. Some of the rocks have been tumbled by the glacier to a smoothness that glistens when wet. I am surprised to find clumps of macrocystis – a brown kelp that I know from the kelp forests of British Columbia. Surely there are no kelp forests here? I wonder what currents have delivered it to this shore.

Rachael, a gregarious Australian composer, is standing thigh-deep in hip waders, holding the cord from her headphones out over the water, where it dangles to a submerged hydrophone. With her long and wild cherry-red hair, she looks to me like a goddess emerged from the sea. She listens to the underwater sounds of ice. Standing on shore with my camera – taking photos because without snow algae to work on, I don't know what to do – I listen, but hear no hint of the sounds that technology has made audible to Rachael.

The fjord is dense with small icebergs, "bergy bits," closer to the size of buses than skyscrapers. Some are sculpted, some are dirty, others are white like a popsicle you've sucked the colour from, and a few have that eerie blue glow emanating from within, seeming to add light to this grey day.

For much of my life, I yearned to visit the north of my imagination: a romantic, ultimate wilderness of sublime landscapes. My romantic view was tempered when I eventually learned about colonialism: residential schools, resource extraction, and global warming. And yet, it is still true that my favourite book as a child was Farley Mowat's *Never Cry Wolf* and that my great-grandfather was in the gold rush.

When I was a child, neither my grandmother, Mary Quarmby, nor my father, Alan, were forthcoming with stories. Both quietly modelled independence and self-sufficiency: Mary raised her two children on her own in a small shack with a woodstove for cooking and no indoor plumbing. (I loved using the hand pump in the yard to pump water from the well for my grandma.) Mary was a woman of few words, and the same remains true of Alan. Mary certainly didn't talk about the mental state of her husband, my grandfather, Lawrence Quarmby, who experienced the worst of trench warfare as a private in the First World War. When Alan and his sister were very young, Lawrence was committed to Essondale Hospital for his PTSD (then known as shell shock). These must have been harrowing times – I have no stories, only echoes and reverberations – and in the midst of losing her husband, Mary lost her father, Arthur Bird.

In 1898, Arthur Bird set off for the Klondike in search of gold. His wife, Louisa, followed with then two-year-old Mary, and the family settled in Dawson City, Yukon Territory. My grandmother thrived and many years later told of panning her own claim near her father's stake. But neither struck it rich and in 1911 the family moved to Victoria, British Columbia, where Arthur returned to his trade as a carpenter. From my reading, many who experienced the gold rush forever after felt the call to return north. As the story goes, it was the depression following the 1929 market crash that gave Arthur the opportunity to go north again, this time for a construction job at Fort Simpson. In *Miners and Moonshiners*, Fred J. Peet writes of "this man whom I knew fairly well":

> He heard of the mining boom at Great Bear Lake. In 1932 he built a small boat and with a few supplies drifted down the Mackenzie River and poled his way up the Bear River to Great Bear Lake. At this time he would be 67 years of age, a loner, he still thought he could strike it rich. A resourceful, independent man, instead of hitching a ride across Great Bear Lake and wary of the danger of storms, he poled his small craft around the south shore a distance of hundreds of miles. Wherever he stopped, he examined the shoreline formations and outcroppings. One of these occasions he found a large seam of hard coal in the sediments about 120 miles from Cameron Bay. He continued on to Cameron Bay and spent the next two years carpentering or prospecting in this area, ever mindful of the coal he had found over 100 miles away.

Arthur was not alone on the journey down the Mackenzie River and around the south shore of Great Bear Lake. He was accompanied by his son George. Years later, George regaled the family with stories of building the small wooden punt, which father and son then propelled along the shore with a pole. When Alan was a young man with a new baby of his own at home (me), he was on a hunting trip with his uncle when George had a heart attack. George died while Alan was driving him to the hospital. This was not part of the family history I grew up with; I learned of it only a few months ago.

Peet continues with Arthur's story:

> During the sports day, August 3, 1934, he told me he thought there would be a demand for this coal as fuel, if the mines developed. He reasoned the slow growing timber in the area would soon be consumed and some other source of fuel would be needed. He must have left his cabin at Cameron Bay soon after the sports day. He had bought four traps from Andy Reid of the Hudson's Bay Company on August 24th. Besides flour and rice, he had bought very little food to last him any length of time, or else he intended living off the land … When his family didn't hear from him at Christmas, they contacted the … RCMP [Royal Canadian Mounted Police] … Chartering Harry Hayter's plane they made a check of the south shore and found the empty cabin, barren of food.

My great-grandfather disappeared into the wilderness of Great Bear Lake in the winter of 1935 – he was seventy and his grandson, Alan, had just turned two. Arthur's diary, which was found in the cabin, reveals that some illness – a bad cold or perhaps the flu – kept him trapped too long in his cabin. Winter arrived, together with hunger, loneliness, and depression. In an act of desperation, he set off to hike out and was never seen again.

My family has a photo of Arthur standing in front of one of his cabins, snow piled high all around. Reading the books, the old letters, Arthur's final diary, and the RCMP letter to Louisa reporting their search and failure to find him, it seems like another world in a long-ago past. But it has been less than one hundred years. It has been no time at all.

I was in my thirties when I learned the story of Arthur's disappearance. As a child, I heard only snippets about the gold rush and my great-grandfather. I knew that my father yearned to go north and find his grandfather's stake. Only recently have I begun to appreciate what a mythic figure Arthur must have been to my fatherless father. Alan quit school before grade eight to support his mother and sister by pulling the green chain at a local sawmill. While he didn't tell many stories, my father taught me about rafts, and poling, and self-sufficiency. Almost by osmosis, I was infused with a longing for adventure, wilderness and the North.

I remember clearly, ten years old, carrying a Second World War army surplus bag. In the bag is my lunch – a lemon cheese sandwich on white bread, an apple, and a homemade chocolate chip cookie. I am alone. I've hiked about a mile from home, down the railway tracks to a small pond that I am pretty sure no adult knows about. On a previous expedition, I'd been here with other kids and we'd hammered together scraps of wood into a semblance of a raft. I am sitting on the ground, watching and listening as a bumblebee visits a clover flower. I am wondering whether the raft will float well enough for me to pole my way – north – across to the other side of the pond. I wade into the water, my toes squishing through the muck, to pull the raft off shore. This is more difficult than I expected, but eventually the raft floats free of shore. I am only shin-deep when I step onto the raft and find myself standing on a raft that is resting on the bottom. I want to tell my disappointed ten-year-old self that it is okay, one day I will travel to the far north on a beautiful ship. I want to remind my almost-sixty-year-old self that after all of these years, I am finally here. Be present.

It's nearing time to return to the *Antigua*, but first, a swim! During orientation, Captain Joe had given us a stern warning about the risks of falling overboard: "After three minutes in water this cold your muscles won't work. You won't be able to swim." Meanwhile, our guide Sarah had effused about the pleasures of an Arctic swim. Sarah advised us not to wear swimsuits "because they slow down the warming up after the swim." She also recommended wearing wool socks into the water. "Most importantly, when you get out, naked but for your wool socks, pay attention to your feet first. Take off the wet socks and put on dry ones. Only then towel dry and dress."

I have both towel and dry socks in my backpack, yet still I'm caught off guard by the idea that now is the time. We're assembling to be shuttled back to the *Antigua* when suddenly everyone is talking about a swim. What, here? Now? With all of these bergy bits floating in the water? I look around for Sarah; she isn't on shore. There must be a mistake. Not here, not now.

I hesitate and then quickly decide yes, I can do this; I want to do this. I find a rock on which to pile my clothes and start stripping. About a dozen of us are spread along the beach, preparing to plunge into ice water. I notice that I am at the edge of the row of swimmers and on the other side of me are the fully clothed non-swimming observers. Some of them have cameras. I grab my stuff and start to move down the beach in a sudden attack of shyness. Hailey is next to me and as I pass her, she becomes the one closest to the cameras. "Wait!" she says. "Where are you going? Don't leave me here." Others are going in. I stop next to Hailey, who is already half undressed. I need to move quickly or I'll be standing on the shore alone and naked. I strip down to my wool socks, tossing my clothes in a pile on the muddy gravel.

I rush to the edge of the water and step in. It's not so bad, with my wool socks on. Another couple of steps and I am up to my knees. Now it is painfully cold and if I were on my own I would go no farther. But there are splashes and squeals as the others go in and I continue on into deeper water. At my thighs; the cold is excruciating. This is dangerous – I could have a heart attack. Suppressing my fear and pain, I keep going. I am up to my belly and my breath catches. Another step and I am chest deep. Instead of going any deeper, I squat so that the water is up to my neck. I look around – for perhaps three seconds. There is no way I am going to put my head under. I turn and rush back out of the iceberg-laden seawater.

On shore, I feel a surge of happiness – I'm falling in love with ice! Ah, the beautiful power of an endorphin rush! Calmly, methodically, and with a smile, I follow Sarah's recommended routine, no longer concerned about being naked among these strange new friends as I carefully dry my feet and pull on fresh wool socks. I enjoy the feel of the towel on my skin, the slight scratchiness of the dry wool socks. What magical concoction of chemicals has this "swim" released? I feel no pain. My skin feels exquisite as I dress. I am euphoric. Endorphins, epinephrine, dopamine, serotonin.

A bliss built from cascades of cellular signals triggered by the excitement and by the cold. Back on the ship I'm still feeling warm and exhilarated as we toast the adventure with Aquavit. It is the beginning of belonging, a scientist among artists.

SCIENTIST

Studying snow algae is new for me. For years, in my lab at Simon Fraser University (near Vancouver, Canada), I studied the biology of a single-celled alga that gives a summertime-green tinge to freshwater puddles and ponds. The microscopic *Chlamydomonas* cells swim by the synchronized beating of two cilia – long, whip-like structures that poke out of the top of the cell and pull the cell forward. Think of a breaststroke: a wide sweep pushes back against the water and a narrow recovery stroke repositions the cilia for another power stroke. They swim to find the sweet spot in the water column: enough light for photosynthesis, but not so much that they suffer from the damaging UV rays.

With slightly offset cilia, the cell swims in a corkscrew pattern, allowing a pigmented region on one side of the cell – the eyespot – to detect the direction and intensity of light with each rotation of the cell. It's a bit like radar: *beep* … (rotation) … *beep* … Or, *BEEP* … (rotation) … *BEEP*! It is mysteries all the way down – answer one question and another emerges, even in this simple example of how a microscopic cell navigates in a pond.

My work was about how the cilia are taken apart and rebuilt. At the end of every day, *Chlamydomonas* disassemble their cilia and absorb the molecules back into the cell. After they've spent the day photosynthesizing and growing, the cells divide overnight. What was one cell at sunset could be two or four or even eight cells by sunrise, depending on how favourable the conditions for growth were on the previous day. Each "daughter" cell grows a new pair of cilia in time to swim to the morning light.

For thirty years I studied how the cilia are disassembled each evening. I know the focus may sound absurdly narrow, but my group used the tools of genetics, molecular biology, biochemistry, and cell biology to identify the cellular machinery controlling disassembly of cilia. The work is meaningful because cilia are ancient cellular structures (their building blocks and organization conserved from *Chlamydomonas* to humans), and much of what we learned by studying them informed us about human biology in health and disease. From decades of focused study, I developed an intuition for the workings of cilia. I loved being a cell biologist.

I mourn the loss of my cell biology research program. To be sure, there were difficult times and the struggle to stay funded was stressful. But oh, the thrill of it! I remember one day when a PhD student, Laura Hilton, drew me out of my office where I'd been immersed in writing a grant proposal ...

Laura wants me to come to the lab, but won't tell me what's going on. "I want you to see for yourself," she says.

I sit down at the microscope and she hands me a slide: "This is cnk2." Cnk2 is the name of a mutant strain of single-celled algae created in my lab. The tiny algal cells have cilia slightly longer than normal. I take a look through the microscope and calibrate my eye to the size of things at this magnification.

Standing beside me, Laura hands me another slide: "This is lf-4." Lf-4 cells have mutant cilia many times longer than normal. Lf-4 cells have been studied for years and the consensus in the field is that this is as long as the cilia of these algal cells can grow. "And this," she says, handing me a third slide, "is the double mutant."

Based on some of her other experiments, Laura had hypothesized that the two genes, cnk2 and lf-4, were working in different pathways, and she predicted that the double mutant cells should have cilia longer than the single mutant lf-4 cells. However, because lf-4 cilia are already at the limits of how long the algal cilia can grow, we were expecting the cilia to approximate the length of lf-4 cells. This was one of those routine experiments that had to be done to make sure that the world was working as we thought.

I set up the slide, and look up at Laura – her face tells me nothing. I turn back to the eyepiece. I am stunned by what I see. I hold my breath and move the microscope stage, scanning the slide. I look at more cells and process what I am seeing. Finally, I push my chair back from the microscope and again look up at Laura. This time she is beaming. I grin and we both start laughing.

"Those cilia are outrageous!" I say.

"I know, eh? They look like spaghetti noodles. I could hardly believe it when I first saw them."

When long-established dogma is overturned, it is a good day in the lab.

While I was happily studying pond scum, the urgency of global warming slowly seeped into my awareness. Although I had read *Heat* by George Monbiot and seen Al Gore's *An Inconvenient Truth*, I still believed governments would do their jobs – that they would act on climate with the necessary regulatory and legislative changes. I was content to leave them to their work and continue with mine. For too long I trusted that we would see governmental action, as we saw on ozone depletion in 1987 with the Montreal Protocol, and on acid rain with regulations put in place throughout the 1980s and 1990s. It was a long time before I finally accepted that those in power were not willing to help human civilization move rapidly away from fossil fuels.

In June 2011, I was in Copenhagen to give an invited research seminar. On a walking tour of the city with my host, Lotte Pedersen, we came upon an outdoor exhibit of larger-than-life photographs of the 2009 protests at the global climate summit. I'd seen photographs of the protests in the news at the time, but being in the same streets, amidst these large images, I felt the anguish of the protesters. I was nauseated by the brutality of the police. By this time, I knew enough about the science of climate change to identify with the intense emotions of those being sprayed with tear gas, beaten with batons, or handcuffed face down on the street. What were we up against? What was the source of such powerful opposition to changes necessary to maintain human rights, social stability, and protection of the environment that sustains us all?

As my anger (and fear) grew, I wrote letters, signed petitions, and attended marches. My engagement in the struggle for climate action escalated, and after a few years – for the first time in over twenty years – I found myself with no research funding.

There is always a tension between the cost of doing science (that is, the research grants that cover salaries, supplies, and equipment) and society's return on its investment. Science, by definition, is an exploration of the unknown – we don't know what we are going to find. Every time science reveals something new, it also exposes a world of questions we hadn't known to wonder about. Curiosity drew me to science. Science, like art, nourishes our humanity. But today, doing science is considerably more expensive than doing art. Commensurate with the greater expense is a greater expectation of accountability. Society invests in science because we know that some investigations will produce impactful discoveries, even if we can't predict which specific lines of investigation will be fruitful. Unfortunately, my tenure in science coincided with the rise of free-market capitalism – neoliberalism – and its ever-increasing demands for directly accountable paybacks.

By the time 2011 arrived, I was struggling to keep my research program funded. I scored just below the funding line with my first application for renewal of my CIHR (Canadian Institutes of Health Research) grant. The review panel noted that my research plans were too far removed from potential clinical application – this in spite of our recent discovery relevant to the causes of polycystic kidney disease. When my application to the CIHR failed for a second time and the review panel suggested I focus my work on kidney cells instead of microscopic algae, I resisted. I wanted to leave that work to the kidney researchers while I continued to probe the cell biology of algae, believing we had yet more unexpected and meaningful discoveries to make. Historically, the most transformative discoveries have come from the most unexpected explorations. There are moments when I wish I had adapted and persevered. It was a failure of confidence, but also, I had lost my drive for the work.

To succeed in this demanding, competitive world requires one's full attention. It is what you think about in the shower. I grew up in blue-collar, rural British Columbia. There was no political discussion around our family dinner table. I had no idea what it meant to be a research scientist, and I did not know being an academic was a thing. Work was physical and reading was subversive: "Put down that book and go do something useful." It was a childhood spent out of doors, poking about in forests, streams, and tide pools. Loving nature was like breathing. Then, in my late twenties, while working at the University of British Columbia as a lecturer of first year biology – after earning a BSc in marine biology and an MSc in oceanography from that same institution – I saw a film loop of an onion cell dividing.

I watched the chromosomes condense and align at the metaphase plate, and then – in one elegant, coordinated motion – half of each chromosome was mysteriously propelled to one pole while the other was whisked to the opposite pole as the cell divided. I played the loop over and over, and marvelled at how a tiny sac of molecules could organize itself and accomplish this beautifully choreographed ballet. In that moment began an arduous, fourteen-year journey to opening my own cell biology research lab.

I ache when I recall the years of my son's childhood when I was obsessing about a grant deadline instead of focusing on him. I want to go back and be there for him. But in those years, I was striving to keep my job. By 2011, things were different. My son was grown and I was defiantly opposed to neoliberalism – the free-market ideology driving the relentless pursuit of growth and wealth, and climate change. I had more important work to do than push the envelope of the unknown. I did not submit a third application for renewal to the CIHR.

I also held an NSERC (Natural Sciences and Engineering Research Council of Canada) grant, specifically for curiosity-driven research. In real dollars, NSERC grants have shrunk dramatically over the years. Many of the funds that do flow to NSERC are now committed to partnership programs – tie your research to the R&D of a company and we'll fund you. For a few years, I tried to do molecular cell biology on my small NSERC grant, but it was simply not enough to support graduate students and expensive molecular reagents. In 2015, after several years as an activist, instead of applying for renewal of my NSERC grant, I ran as a candidate in the Canadian federal election.

By the time I lost the election, I was burned out from activism and the negativity of politics. I longed to immerse myself once again in science, to puzzle over fresh data, pulling meaning from the shape of a curve, the colours on a heat map, the location of proteins within a cell, but I had no funding. At the same time, I continued to feel a strong pull to do everything possible to shift the destructive path of human activity. Here I was in my fifties, asking questions about my place in the world. I was starting over.

When I finally awoke to the urgency of global warming, molecular cell biology began to feel like a luxury we couldn't afford.

Although I knew the long-term potential of my cellular work – that it could lead to cures or treatments of diseases – once I understood the singular geological moment that defined my lifetime, I couldn't turn away. I wanted to understand the impacts of global warming on the biology of Earth. I wanted to help avert the worst. Above all, I wanted to find a way forward that played to my strengths.

A serendipitous meeting with Forest Rohwer, a biologist who studies the ecology of viruses, provided a resolution. We were both attending a cell biology conference in San Diego, and after we discussed his work on the gut microbiome (he had presented one of the major symposium talks and I sought him out with my questions), Forest asked about my science. I described my dilemma and he responded with a story about snow algae and climate change. Here was a project that offered an unanticipated opportunity to apply my expertise in the cell biology of microalgae to an ecological system with a direct link to global warming.

Snow algae blooms are a rich microbiome of diverse microscopic organisms, including fungi, rotifers, tardigrades, ciliates, snow fleas, bacteria, archaea, and viruses, but it is the algae that are responsible for the distinctive red colour. The normally green cells synthesize high levels of a red pigment, which serves as a sunscreen and transforms the cells into microscopic rubies. Blooms develop to such high cell densities that the snow can become a strong red – so-called watermelon snow. These red patches of snow absorb solar energy, causing further melting. Because growth of the microbes is limited by a lack of liquid water, this enhanced warming and melting fosters further growth. In this way, the snow algae establish a positive feedback loop that amplifies local warming and accelerates the seasonal melt of the snowfields. As the extent and seasonal duration of snow and ice coverage diminishes with global warming, there are indications of algal blooms on an increasing fraction of remaining snowfields.

Forest had done a project on watermelon snow collected from Franz Josef Land, an archipelago in the Russian high Arctic. Svalbard is at almost the same latitude as Franz Josef Land. Within two months of meeting Forest, I submitted my application to join the Arctic Circle residency. I'd had my eye on this residency since my artist friend Hannah Campbell had been on it a few years earlier, and now, here was my opportunity.

In the eighteen months between applying to the residency and arriving on the tall ship *Antigua*, I learned a great deal about snow algae, including the important fact that they are abundant in alpine snowfields within two hours of my lab. The summer before the expedition, I initiated a project in our local mountains and received an NSERC grant to study alpine snow algae.

And so by the time I arrived in Svalbard, the stakes for finding watermelon snow in the Arctic weren't as high as they would otherwise have been. Or rather, the stakes were still high, just different. Acutely aware of the paradox of extinction tourism – travelling to experience something before it's gone, and, in making the trip, contributing to the demise of the very thing one travelled to see – I still needed to believe I would produce something worthwhile from this trip. Fleetingly, I wished it could be enough that going North was something I'd dreamed about since I was a child. But in the end, it is all about stories and I need a better one.

ON WHY STORIES MATTER

Svalbard remained more or less free of humanity until the seventeenth century, when Europeans and Russians began arriving in significant numbers as whalers and miners, explorers and adventurers, artists and scientists. Few people have stayed for a lifetime, most for much less. It's a place without stories indigenous to the land.

I travelled here from Coast Salish territory on the west coast of North America, just north of the forty-ninth parallel. Coast Salish territory includes Vancouver, Canada, and the southeast coast of Vancouver Island, where I grew up. This territory has been my family's home for four generations, over one hundred years. It has been the home of the Coast Salish people and their relations – all of the natural world – for countless generations, thousands of years. They are rooted in the land, a deep belonging. Those who survived colonial genocide are emerging from oppression and finding their voices. Settlers, like me, have a lot of listening to do.

Thomas King, an "American-Canadian of Cherokee, German and Greek descent," tells two creation myths in his book *The Truth about Stories*. After telling the stories, King shows how although both tell about the creation of the world, they are very different stories. One, from Genesis, describes a world ruled by hierarchies. God is all-powerful and man rules over nature. It's a myth that "celebrates law, order, and good governance." In contrast, the Woman Who Fell from the Sky is a story filled with creatures that work together. The powers of deities are limited, mistakes are made, there is humour, and finding balance is key. The contrast King illuminates is in the world we inherit through story – a world of opposition and competition, or one of cooperation and harmony. To paraphrase King, we can change the world with the stories we listen to and the stories we tell. Given the mess we're in, King wonders, "Did we just start out with the wrong story?"

What is my story? I am a biologist, so a major frame for me is evolution. In his preface to *On the Origin of Species* (1859), Darwin writes:

> Although much remains obscure, and will long remain obscure, I can entertain no doubt, after the most deliberate study and dispassionate judgment of which I am capable, that the view which most naturalists until recently entertained, and which I formerly entertained – namely, that each species has been independently created – is erroneous.

Into a culture permeated with Genesis, a new story was born. Twelve years later in his introduction to *The Descent of Man*, Darwin writes:

> I collected notes on the origin or descent of man, without any intention of publishing on the subject, but rather with the determination not to publish, as I thought that I should thus only add to the prejudices against my views. It seemed to me sufficient to indicate, in the first edition of my 'Origin of Species,' that by this work "light would be thrown on the origin of man and his history;" and this implies that man must be included with other organic beings in any general conclusion respecting his manner of appearance on this earth.

Even as natural selection and evolution slowly assumed cultural sway (in most of the world), bolstered by countless scientific studies, refinements, and fresh examples, Darwin's ideas were twisted by some into a defense of power and dominance that preserved the hierarchical worldview of Genesis. But natural selection and evolution are not in any way linked to that particular origin myth.

Three things we know that Darwin did not:

1 As bizarre as it sounds, the information of heredity, the code
from which all life is built, is a simple linear sequence of four
molecules, known as G, C, A, and T, the nucleotides. These
molecules link together in long chains to form DNA. How
can a language of only four letters encode the blueprints for
something as complex as life? The solution is ingenious. The
ribosome, an ancient molecular machine found in every living
cell on Earth, reads the linear code three letters at a time.
The three-letter sequences are then translated into a linked
chain of amino acids, forming proteins. For example, the
sequence ATGCATGGA would be read as ATG-CAT-GGA and
translated into methionine-histidine-glycine. There are over
twenty different amino acids, each with a different shape and
chemical character. Each particular sequence of amino acids,
or protein, folds into its characteristic shape – a shape that may,
for example, catalyze an essential cellular reaction, or, like the
sugar receptors on the surface of *E. coli*, sense the presence of
another molecule. In this way, DNA encodes a startling array
of tens of thousands of different proteins, each with its unique
properties and cellular functions. From a vocabulary of four
letters and the grammar of chemistry, evolution discovered the
rich three-dimensional language of life.

2 By comparing the DNA sequences from different organisms,
especially the stretches that encode basic component parts
like those involved in sensing the environment or metabolism,
one can see patterns of heredity emerge. Careful analysis of a
mind-boggling quantity of high-quality data has revealed that
all extant life on Earth has been evolving for close to the same
length of time, about four billion years. For about half of that
time, we were all microbes. There is no higher and lower, no
more recently evolved, no lesser beings, no hierarchy. We aren't
descended from the apes; rather, we and the apes are descended
from a common ancestor, and so on. Life has radiated out from
one ancient ancestor. We are all related.

3 Given that we're all related and have been interacting with one another for a very long time, it should come as no surprise that the deeper we go with our scientific explorations, the more we discover that ecological connections between species are complex and often intimate. Even species that haven't shared an ancestor for a billion years are found entwined in more co-dependent relationships than Darwin could have imagined. With varying degrees of separation, our lives are all connected.

"Survival of the fittest" provides only a narrow view of our origins. Life is not a zero-sum game. Mutualisms emerge and life expands into previously unavailable niches. The natural world is replete with cooperation and sometimes harmony.

EXPEDITION

Once again, we travelled north through the night and are now anchored near another glacier, Smeerenburgbreen – "Whale Blubber Glacier." Like yesterday, the morning is foggy and the air is still, but strangely, the water isn't flat and reflective. At first I don't understand what I'm looking at through the fog, but then I see the surface is broken everywhere with ice, ice of all sizes, baseball- and toaster-size chunks of ice, and an occasional car- or school bus-size bergy bit, all chunky and jagged. The only flat surfaces are small patches of open water. The air is thick with fog that floats and drifts, dissipates and reforms. This is the fog that filmmakers try to emulate with their fog machines, to set the mood for suspense and a sense of foreboding, something lurking just out of sight, sounds muffled.

In the Zodiacs, we tour slowly along the face of the glacier. As we drift through the fog the ice tinkles, a massive, cathedral-worthy tinkle. Sound artist, Rachael captures what we are hearing in a phrase: "Cocktail party at the end of the world." We are drifting, the fog is drifting, and the chunks of ice all around us are drifting. Landmarks appear and disappear. I breathe the fog. We are all quiet, listening to the ice. A coy promontory with sculpted rocks and pillows of snow appears and then hides, but doesn't quite disappear, like a young child playing peek-a-boo. The looming face of the glacier reveals its undulating layers, and a large cave looms where the layers below a particular undulation have collapsed.

Smeerenburgbreen is crumbling into the sea. Occasionally, gulls resting on bergy bits floating near the glacier rise suddenly, as we saw yesterday, exploding up and away, an early warning system for what follows in a beat – the loud crack of cleaving, the birth of a bergy bit. The calving is accompanied by clouds of white ice raining down into the sea, followed by dramatic fountains of splash. We ride the waves. Those of the crew who know this place tell us they've never seen so much activity, such big calves.

We approach the glacier and I can see that the thousands of birds are blacklegged kittiwakes. They dive just below the surface of the water, feeding on plankton and small fish. Between dives they ride on the drifting bergy bits like patient commuters on a downtown bus. Occasionally one flies off while the others barely notice. The kittiwakes are evidence of an invisible productivity. What I know but don't see: the melting glacier is fertilizing the sea, releasing nutrients like nitrogen (N), phosphorus (P), sulphur (S), and iron (Fe) that have been trapped in the ice, allowing the algae to make best use of constant daylight, to grow and capture nutrients that will cycle through the complex community of interacting, cooperating microscopic organisms, the plankton.

We tend to think of ourselves as more highly evolved than, well, everything else – certainly plankton. Once again our ancient stories are at play and our psychology lags behind our scientific knowledge that every living thing has an evolutionary history as long as ours. We confuse evolutionary longevity with complexity. While we are no more highly evolved than any other being on Earth, we are arguably the most complex beings in an evolutionary lineage that specializes in complexity (the eukaryotes). The complexity of the human brain – the number and types of cells and molecules, each interacting in networks of local, context-dependent ways such that emergent properties arise – underlies the creativity and inventiveness that has produced a human world so complex that none of us can comprehend the totality of civilization.

ON EVOLVING WITH OTHERS

I am sustained by Nature and her stories. For me, learning about Nature has fostered a worldview that embraces science and romance, technology and collaboration, gratitude and reverence. I cherish stories about our ancestors. They have much to tell us about our place in the world.

Around two billion years ago, by a process that seems to have involved some early cells engulfing other early cells and all of them coming to live in peaceful coexistence, the eukaryotic lineage was born. Eukaryotic cells are larger and considerably more complex than prokaryotic cells such as *E. coli*, the engulfed cell having since become mitochondria. Perhaps due to a new energy efficiency bestowed by mitochondria, the eukaryotes blossomed with innovations, including multicellularity, the cornerstone of organisms like us, built of many different types of cells.

Among the plankton is a eukaryotic cell that might reveal how multicellularity developed in animals. Most of the time, choanoflagellates are single-cell organisms with a distinctive collar that looks a bit like one of those cones a pet cat or dog might wear to keep them from chewing on a bandage. Unlike the pet collar, the choanoflagellate collar isn't solid, but rather is porous and allows water to flow through its delicate fringe-like structure. Protruding from the middle of the collar and extending way out into the water is a solitary, elegant cilium, which creates a flow to the collar where bacteria are captured and eaten. Sometimes, choanoflagellate cells stay together after cell division, forming small colonies known as rosettes. These are rudimentary multicellular organisms.

The pioneering scientific team in this field, led by Nicole King at UC Berkeley, discovered that choanoflagellates carry in their DNA copies of the same genes that are key for animal multicellular existence. The choanoflagellates grow well as single cells in the lab, but only rarely form the colonial rosettes. This meant there was little the group could do to use this "single cell to colony" switch as a proxy to study an early stage in the evolution of multicellular animals.

Serendipitously, an attentive student noticed that when they cleaned up their cultures by treating with a mix of antibiotics, the choanoflagellates did not form any rosettes at all. The group got to work and from a series of careful experiments, they determined that a species of bacteria secretes a complex of compounds that trigger the formation of colonies by the choanoflagellates.

This is a stunning discovery: Cross-kingdom communication dictates the growth form of a complex single-celled eukaryote. At first it seems strange that one species would control the development of another, until you remember the deep interconnectedness of all life on Earth. The regulation of choanoflagellates by signals from a bacterium is giving us new ways to think about how the microbes living in our gut and on our skin are affecting the health and wellbeing of humans. For now, it's still strange for us to think about complex organisms being "controlled" by bacteria.

The choanoflagellate story gets even weirder. One more time, serendipity visited this group of prepared minds. While looking for something else entirely, the team discovered that a very different molecule secreted by yet another species of bacteria induced the choanoflagellates to have sex. The group named the molecule (an enzyme) EroS, for Extracellular regulator of Sex.

Sex? Sex to a biologist: the formation of gametes (sperm and egg, for example) by meiosis, followed by the fusion of gametes from different parents, and the development of an individual that is a hybrid of the parents. Clues such as the presence of genes for meiosis tell us that most, if not all eukaryotes we discover in nature probably reproduce sexually. But for most organisms, this is rarely if ever observed in the lab. Most of the time, when we can get things to grow at all, the cells simply divide and produce copies of the original, what we call asexual division. To get a species to reproduce sexually in the lab is a big deal. To discover that the key to sex is a protein secreted by an organism from a different kingdom is huge! (And weird.)

The discovery of EroS raises a lot of questions, such as: Why? What is in it for the bacteria? Secreting a protein is expensive and not something done without benefit for the organism doing the secreting. Perhaps choanoflagellates undergoing sexual reproduction in some way create an environment more favourable to the bacteria? Or perhaps, from the perspective of the bacteria, secreting the protein has nothing to do with choanoflagellates. From the perspective of the choanoflagellates, is there something about the presence of this bacteria and its secreted protein that would make it advantageous to undergo a round of sexual reproduction? Does the presence of EroS correlate with a change in the environment for which the recombination of sexual reproduction might by chance offer an appropriate adaptation via a shuffling of the cards?

In the wild, choanoflagellates live with hundreds or possibly thousands of different species of bacteria – not to mention algae, archaea, all sorts of ciliates, fungi, and viruses. To what extent are these various organisms communicating and reacting to one another's presence?

There is so much we don't know. Science excels at revealing the expanse of what is unknown. For every question answered, many more are raised. At the same time, our scientific knowledge of the world is significant and growing. Scientists understand the physics of global warming and are learning how the complex patterns of Earth's climate are changing in response to the warming of both the atmosphere and the oceans. To understand is to be able to make predictions. Scientists can make reliable predictions about the relationships between the amount of greenhouse gas in the atmosphere, global mean temperature, and sea level. What is much harder to predict is whether humanity will successfully rise against what I call the cheater class – those who are rich, powerful, and callous enough to continue pushing fossil fuels for their own gains. Cheating is an evolutionary strategy that may serve the individual and his genes, but if the cheaters come to dominate, the species may be doomed.

EXPEDITION

It's afternoon. The *Antigua* remains at anchor in front of Smeerenburgbreen while we're ferried by Zodiac from the ship to a hilly island. We disembark onto boulders and scramble up the slope, trying to stay on rocks or snow because walking on the soil risks damage to the sparse and slow-growing plants. One misstep and I'm into mud eight inches deep. I use snow to wash the evidence of this misdemeanour from my boot and strive more diligently to find a solid path in search of pink snow. It doesn't take long to determine there is only white (and now some muddy) snow on this small island. I'm disappointed. I felt sure this was going to be the place.

I take some photographs. The *Antigua* looks impossibly small at anchor in front of the glacier. Beth, a young contemporary dance artist from Surrey, UK, has her camera on a tripod and is recording herself repeatedly "practicing falling." She's on the edge of a steep slope and I can see that the background must be stunning – an expanse of sea with large bergy bits and a sky filled with thick, creamy clouds, slate blue, grey, and white swirled together, sharp divisions between one cloud and the next, as though each is outlined in pencil. I imagine in her videos it must look as though she is falling through this surreal sky.

I climb a little higher and on the summit I find that Emma has enlisted one of our guides to assist her. Benja, from Patagonia and among the youngest on this trip, has set aside his rifle to lie on his back and hold up a piece of knitting. Emma asks, "Will you join us?" I am, of course, happy to help, but I'm nervous about messing up her work. Benja looks relaxed, as though assisting highly accomplished artists is old hat. Emma asks me to capture the video as she pulls a thread to unravel the fabric, revealing the glacier behind. I'm feeling like a total imposter. I've been hiding behind my camera, but I'm no photographer. "No, no, don't worry, you'll do fine," Emma soothes. "Whatever you get will be fine. I think the problem will be the fabric. It might be too tightly knit. Let's just see what we get." I remain nervous and struggle to maintain a tight frame on the knitting, slowly shifting the focus from fabric to glacier in sync with the unravelling. Unravelling. Earth's systems are unravelling. In this project Emma is contrasting the time it takes to make things with the time it takes to consume them. "Unravelling" is another of several projects that occupy Emma on this trip.

I watch as Lucy spreads and anchors lengths of pre-cut metallized plastic film (think Mylar) to form a disc of about four metres in diameter over the snow. Lucy, an architect from Sydney, Australia, does public art and "creative public infrastructure." I've been curious about her project for this trip since seeing a photo of one of her sculptures installed by the sea in Sydney: a one-and-a-half-metre diameter acrylic globe filled with water forms a lens through which the beach, ocean, sky, and the Sydney skyline are viewed upside down. The shiny disc on the snow in front of me is decorated with a pattern of semicircular cuts, allowing the wind to flow through without the sheets blowing away. It sparkles and quivers on the snow. Lucy struggles to unfurl the film. I work my way down the hill and am ready to offer my assistance when she gets it pinned down.

I'm here to work with artists to find ways of inspiring real action on global warming and Lucy's project is explicitly focused on global warming. Her view is that artists have more freedom than scientists to play with ideas. I'm not convinced, but I listen. Her basic idea is scientifically sound: the metallized plastic will reflect solar radiation back into space, reducing the amount of heat absorbed by the earth. As snow and ice melt, the darker surfaces of rock and water are exposed. Less radiation is reflected, more heat absorbed, and global warming is accelerated. Lucy's goal is to slow the melting of the snow. I wonder whether, in a real-world implementation, the metallized plastic sheet would be installed over rock or water, not white snow (which is already doing a good job of reflecting radiation), but this is an art project, not geoengineering. I wonder about the environmental cost of the metallized plastic, both its synthesis and its disposal, but at this point, everything about global warming is a trade-off, and Lucy's project is about provoking ideas. In truth, I'm offended by the hubris of geoengineering, and Lucy's art project makes me uncomfortable.

There are two general approaches to geoengineering for climate change – those designed to reduce warming, and those that would "scrub" carbon dioxide from the atmosphere. Approaches to reducing warming include spraying aerosols into the atmosphere to reflect incoming radiation. Lucy's metalized plastic would also reduce warming, but with different side effects – for example, plastic pollution and an impact on the underlying ecosystem. Most importantly, even if we successfully reflect enough solar radiation with approaches like these, we're left with an excess of atmospheric carbon dioxide that is dissolving in and acidifying the oceans to toxic levels. The pH of our oceans is already 30 per cent more acidic than it was in pre-industrial times.

Approaches to removing carbon dioxide, so-called negative emissions or carbon capture and storage, have potential, but so far the technology is either insane (for example, fertilizing the oceans so planktonic algae do more photosynthesis, upsetting entire oceanic ecosystems in the process) or enormously expensive, risky, and yet to be established as feasible for scale-up (for example, chemical carbon capture). To be clear, I'm all in favour of continuing to develop carbon capture technology; it has potential and ultimately costs will come down. We need it as part of our repertoire, but at best it will be part of the answer.

Why would we put so much emphasis on geoengineering when there are so many alternative approaches that are affordable and don't involve trying to compensate for one form of pollution by adding a new form of pollution? The boreal forests of northern Canada are one of the most important land-based carbon sinks on the planet, and yet we continue to strip away the forests (or poison them from below) to extract the bitumen. Belated appreciation of the urgent need to deal with climate change could lead to panic and a desperate grasping at risky implementations of geoengineering. We're degrading the environment in so many ways that it becomes tedious to recount. Perfecting carbon capture will not rescue rivers polluted with agricultural runoff, and so on. A civilization based on extraction and consumption, with pollution all along the chain, is doomed. Conversely, if we take on the hard work of a speedy and dramatic reduction in greenhouse gas emissions through reduced extraction, reduced consumption, and reuse, it will pay dividends in a healthier environment.

I should have this conversation about geoengineering with Lucy, but I do not. I rationalize to myself that I don't know much about how artists approach problems. Later, I'll recognize the fallacy in my thinking. In the moment, I fail to take the opportunity to talk with a caring and motivated person as she stands on the snow beside me. My discomfort about the difficulty of this conversation is precisely my challenge.

I wonder what I would do if I were a member of the IPCC (the Intergovernmental Panel on Climate Change), charged with informing the world about possible climate futures? The scientists and economists of the IPCC build models – mathematical, computer models that simulate what will happen if we do this or that, continue with business as usual, or begin reducing our emissions on this or that timetable, with this or that change in land use, et cetera.

Here is one scenario: The IPCC warns if humanity continues down the path of business as usual, we can expect a four degrees Celsius increase in global average temperature by the end of the century. Here is the problem with that scenario: As bad as that sounds, the reality for the business-as-usual scenario is worse than a four degrees Celsius temperature increase by 2100. All IPCC scenarios of recent years soften the blow by including optimistic (many would say unrealistic) assumptions about timely and cost-effective implementation of carbon capture and storage. Why is this so bad? It's bad because it gives us the illusion we have more time for adaptation and mitigation than is probably available. Would I tell it straight? Trust people to find their own ways to manage the existential crisis? In the abstract, yes. In the specific – in person – it's more difficult.

The realities of climate change are brutal; I struggle to embrace the truth. I'm overwhelmed by frustration, anger, and discouragement. How could I share with Lucy the harsh truth that the thought of reflecting solar radiation with metallized plastic breaks my heart? I regret not having the conversation with her. I'm confident Lucy could handle the truth – if she doesn't know it already. My reticence arises (in part) from a fear of being perceived as a zealot, a fear of inadequately explaining the rational basis for my opinions. I fantasize about Lucy and me working together to transform her work into a protest that illustrates the folly of trying to solve one form of pollution with another. I see us planting protest signs in the snow next to her shiny disc, "Circular Economies Not Shiny Discs!" "Save the Microbes!"

I make my way slowly down the hill to await a Zodiac for the return trip to the *Antigua*. Near the water's edge, in a protected nook, I see Brandy, another of our Canadian contingent, dancing. She's wearing a shaggy white coat and from this distance looks vaguely like a polar bear. I watch, transfixed. Her movements feel mournful. Are mournful. We return to the ship and gather in the salon for dinner. Tacos! We laugh at the juxtaposition of Mexican food in the high Arctic, but enjoy the new flavours. The crew raise the anchor and the *Antigua* continues north.

ON REGRET

A friend claims to have lived her life without regret. I am not impressed. In *Almost Islands*, Stephen Collis quotes his older brother as saying, "When I look back over my life, I don't just see a mountain of regret, I see a whole mountain *range* of regret." Arthur Bird knew something about regret. These diary entries chronicle the final month of his life:

> 30 last of Nov. Quiet and snowing, you can almost hear the flakes drop. Noon Dec. 2. Sun just coming up; cold. 4 (Dec.) 3.30 Near dark, very still and lonesome feel. 5 (Dec.) Grand day, sun out and Chinook wind. 6 Dec. 9.15 a.m. Still dark. Just to tell you its raining and blowing. 8 (Dec.) A plane has just past heading for the coal and I am here. I'll send this if they call coming back. 9 (Dec.) Plane never come back just down to see me, I am near nuts, dark at four o'clock. Flash light good night. 13 (Dec.) 10 a.m. Candle light. No frost and me 15 miles from the coal. I am almost crazy, you no money and me in debt and no meat, flour, beans, sugar & tea; it's tough. 19 (Dec.) 9.00 a.m. Moonlight. This is the worst winter I ever had. What I stayed here for 15 miles to the coal just because I was all in with a cold. I am near crazy for being such a fool. Good-bye. 24 (Dec.) Going to bed. A mild night. Wish I was home. Good-night XX 6.30 Merry Xmas Ma. Xmas day

11 a.m. Lonesome and blue. 31 (Dec.) Hoping our next will
be better dinner, beans, tea, bannock. Cold wind blowing.
1 Jan. 1935. Everything look black. No fur, no money and
near 70 and 120 miles back. Don't think I can make it.

Our global situation as a species is as precarious as Arthur Bird's
individual predicament. Arthur regrets not taking the necessary steps
when he could. Now he is trapped with broken snowshoes, in the dead of
winter, running out of food. He has become a victim of his own mistakes.
Above all, why was he there alone? The delusion of self-sufficiency?

While I have my fair mountain of regrets, when it comes to things
like my gas-guzzling '67 Chevy Impala V8 (used, not then classic) or my
frequent flyer status during my ascent as a young scientist, I regret only
softly and with compassion. I wish I'd engaged sooner with the struggle
to transition off fossil fuels. Do I regret that my climate activism has not
been more effective and that my country continues an aggressive perpetua-
tion of fossil fuel use? Intensely. I agonize over missed opportunities and
ineffective actions.

EXPEDITION

After travelling three hours north from Smeerenburgbreen, the *Antigua* is pushing into the "rotten" fast ice of Fuglefjorden. Rotten is an apt nickname for such ice, tinged green from pockets of air and water, disintegrating. The captain's goal seems to be to wedge us into the ice as a temporary moorage. This is a new vantage on a world that gets stranger the further north we travel. In this fjord the ice is sufficiently solid that we can't approach the glacier by boat, and sufficiently rotten that it doesn't tempt the thought of walking. It's colder here. I pull the zipper of my parka up under my chin and tug up my hood. I peer over the side of the boat and am surprised to see ice forming in the seawater. I watch as the water crystallizes, spreading out from the boat, obviously thin and slushy, but spreading rapidly. The freezing sea is me finding a new grounding – I think I have something, it starts to crystallize, but before it truly gels, things shift and the aspirational solid ground is gone. The *Antigua* pulls out of the ice and continues north.

Two hours north of the rotten fast ice of Fuglefjorden we arrive at the northwestern tip of Spitsbergen and set anchor for the night (79°49′4″N, 11°29′2″E). Heavy clouds hang high in the sky; the lower atmosphere is clear. The water is flat and calm, and the light is blue – mountains blue with distance, a glacier of blue ice, and slate blue water reflecting the dark sky.

Many of our group are on the tiny island of Cummingøya for the morning, but I stay aboard the *Antigua*, nursing lower back pain and sorting photos. There are others who stayed behind and they seem at peace with it. I am not. I'm frustrated at missing the landing, and a foul mood has formed around my back pain, a mood made worse by knowing it's a direct result of packing unwisely. I brought a duffle because I imagined it would be easier to stow on the ship than a rolling suitcase. True enough, but the heavy duffle and daypack with tripod and camera gear were too much for me to lug about on my travels to get here. I recall how judgmental I had been about the bulky kits of the artists. Distracted, I had failed to actually pack until it was time to leave, and the amassed weight of my stuff was an unpleasant and too-late surprise. Packing small is not the same as packing light.

I chat with Hailey, an Australian photographer, and J. Anthony – "call me J" – a composer from Minnesota. They too are struggling. We're all feeling overwhelmed. I'm not alone in having arrived exhausted and finding sleep difficult because of the daily overstimulation. I am also feeling the emotional weight of being here, at the soft heart of global melting.

Several artists in the salon sit quietly with notebooks, sketchpads, or computers. They have stayed aboard, passing on this particular outing for some downtime to process. Jesus, a landscape painter and proud Basque, is at the upper table painting quietly. J turns back to his manuscript paper and is soon lost in thought, occasionally scribbling musical notations. I wonder how his music is being influenced by the ice. Is he writing a lament for the melting glaciers?

Hailey asks, "Would you like me to show you a few tricks in Lightroom?" (This is photo-editing software that I'd learned in a crash course a month before the expedition.) I eagerly accept Hailey's offer. She wants to show me some sophisticated uses of the graduated filter, but I ask, "What makes some photographs art?" Hailey groans but good-naturedly engages me, and together we critique her photos from yesterday.

Later, on the floor in the cabin I share with M, Cara massages my back and teaches me some exercises that will ease my pain.

ON MICROBES AND POLAR BEARS

Almost two centuries before Darwin published *On the Origin of Species*, Antonj van Leeuwenhoek discovered microbes using his simple, hand-held microscope with a lens more refined than those that had come before. I once wrote a villanelle in celebration of Leeuwenhoek.

Antonj van Leeuwenhoek

Under a lens and good light,
the draper viewed threads of linen and wool;
Such wonders he brought to sight.

Tartar from teeth whets his appetite
for microbes that wiggle and swim
under a lens and good light.

In a vial of pond scum was much to delight:
Spirogyra! Volvox! Vorticella!
Such wonders he brought to sight.

Dissections and diagrams, yes Antonj was bright.
Fleas have fleas he discovered,
under a lens and good light.

In pulsing blood flowed the erythrocyte:
Add rainwater – see them explode!
Such wonders he brought to sight.

Shivers and shudders for one parasite;
Yes, it was he discovered the spermatocyte
under a lens and good light.
Such wonders he brought to sight.

No one was prepared for the news that ours is a world dominated by squiggly squirmy things smaller than the eye can see. After initial scepticism, Robert Hooke (discoverer of cells; author of *Micrographia*, 1665) championed Leeuwenhoek's observations, which were published soon thereafter (in 1677). At the time, these microscopic creatures were thought to arise spontaneously from rotting matter, complete little animalcules, with little hearts and little lungs. While those surmises were wrong, the basic facts were correct: the world was filled with microscopic living things that grow and reproduce.

I imagine being a friend of Leeuwenhoek. It's a warm summer day in 1676 and we're sitting by a Delft canal, chatting about how Johannes Vermeer's widow and kids are getting on after his death last year, when Antonj hands me one of his handheld microscopes loaded with a vial of water from the canal. For a while I don't see much of anything at all. I'm about to hand it back to him when a ball of the most gorgeous green cells rolls across my field of view. I sit up straight and attentive.

Before long, an animalcule drifts into view. Its body is transparent and I can see a bright red gut! And it appears to have one foot and two heads and the hair on both heads is waving all around. Bizarre! It's an afternoon of microscopic delights. Over the next several weeks, Antonj shows me many wonders from his microscopic world. I'm one of the privileged few to view this world with my own eyes – it's beautiful. I obsess about what we might look at next, but not once does it cross my mind that what I'm seeing changes my place in the world. It doesn't occur to me that this microscopic world has anything at all to do with the world I live in. I'm more interested in trying to get Antonj to talk about rumours I've heard regarding Johannes's use of lenses and mirrors to make his paintings, but Antonj has made a vow and will not speak of it.

There were few microscopes in existence and if you hadn't actually seen microbes with your own eyes, the whole idea of a microbial world was too bizarre for serious thought. The discovery of microbes had little impact on the thinking of the day.

Popular imagination and scientific attention ignored the existence of microbes until they were connected to human disease. In the mid-nineteenth century, Louis Pasteur developed the germ theory of disease, and Ferdinand Cohn and Robert Koch developed techniques for the isolation and culturing of bacteria. Culturing of isolated strains allowed the identification of specific microbes as the agents of varied and numerous infectious diseases. This medical perspective on microbiology left us with a cramped and negative view of the organisms that hold life together. In two hundred years, microbes progressed from creatures too weird to think about to foul germs. As Darwin suspected and we now know, these microscopic creatures, weird, foul, and otherwise, are our kin.

By the mid-twentieth century, electron microscopy was allowing us to peer beyond the resolution of even the best light microscope. George Palade, one of the founders of the field of cell biology, first noted tiny balls present in every cell examined. As it turned out, these balls are ribosomes – those molecular machines that translate DNA code into proteins. Proteins are the fundamental building blocks of molecular machines. All of life on Earth is made of cells that depend on molecular machines, and every living cell contains ribosomes.

We can compare the sequence of particular sections of DNA to discern the evolutionary relationships in a group of organisms. To get a big-picture view of the major lineages, we sequence something fundamental and ubiquitous, like ribosomes. With sequencing technologies available today, we can compare ribosomal genes from thousands of species. We can sequence pure strains grown in the lab and we can sequence the whole shebang of stuff filtered from a litre of water (or soil or snowmelt).

By comparing the sequences of ribosomal genes, we can draw a single tree of life that includes all known life (including much that is known only as DNA sequence from a sample of soil or sea and never observed as a living cell). This is in contrast to the multiple independent trees Darwin sketched – mosses here, finches there – with no obvious way to connect them. On a quest to understand the deep evolutionary history of the genetic code, Carl Woese sequenced ribosomal RNA from a wide range of microbes, including some from extreme environments. The work revealed a bigger surprise than anyone was expecting – a new category of life. The archaea is a lineage that diverged from bacteria before the eukaryotic lineage was born.

All three of the major lineages of life are represented in microbial communities such as soil, plankton, or watermelon snow. Bacteria and archaea are both prokaryotic, structurally simple cells with no internal membrane-bounded compartments – no wonder that we didn't notice that some of them were wildly different from the rest. Although the cells are small and simple-looking, bacteria and archaea are both rich in bio-chemical diversity, and as communities they have an astounding range of ways of eking out a living and working together in every marginal environment imaginable.

E. coli and the wriggly things Leeuwenhoek found in scrapings from his teeth are bacteria. Methanogens in the guts of cows are examples of archaea (yes, methane from cow farts and burps is really a thing). *Chlamydomonas*, snow algae, choanoflagellates – all of these are examples of eukaryotic microbes. All macroscopic life in our world, from seaweed to polar bears, is in the eukaryotic lineage.

Knowing that we evolved from microbes, that at least half the time we have been evolving was as microbes, that there are more species of microbes than everything else taken together, that we have evolved in the context of microbes and that we are walking human scaffolds teeming with microbes – it changes the way a person sees the world. Microbes tie all life on Earth together; we share evolutionary roots and through microbes we are all functionally connected.

Microbes quite literally modified the geochemistry of Earth in ways that allowed our lineage to emerge – for example, by oxygenating the atmosphere. Microbes are like the webbing that weaves all of Earthly life together – a weaving that has been ongoing for four billion years. Woven more tightly in some places than others, worn through and unravelling a bit in some places, but holding together well enough that some repair work could restore a former glory.

Save the microbes! Yes, but also the polar bears. The lineages of *E. coli* and polar bears are equally old, equally tweaked to become their unique selves. While every extant organism has its four-billion-year saga to tell, some of these stories are more spectacular than others. When polar bears are gone from Earth, I hope their story continues as an evolution into something new. But the rapid rate of change we are currently experiencing – causing – limits the opportunities for evolutionary change. The four-billion-year-long streak of evolutionary tinkering that lead to polar bears is one of many that may be broken by the end of the century.

Extinction is nothing new. At rates that fluctuate, extinctions and speciation are part of life on Earth. Our current accelerated rate of extinction is the sixth time that large numbers of species have gone extinct over a relatively short period. That doesn't make it any less grievous that our species is the cause – pollution, habitat fragmentation and degradation, and now, climate change. Our actions are putting magnificent organisms at risk. I recall a polar bear I saw in a zoo when I was twelve. He was sitting on a fibreglass platform shaped and painted to look like an iceberg. It was a warm summer day and I stood and communed with the sad bear.

EXPEDITION

When the others return from the morning landing on Cummingøya, the crew weighs anchor and we continue north. Here, there is nothing but the Arctic Ocean and its pack ice between the North Pole and us. As the ice-class *Antigua* glides between fragments of broken pack ice, we crowd the decks with our binoculars, cameras, and awe. Because of his own chronic pain, Justin is well stocked with pain meds, and he has shared something robust with me. Now, standing on the deck, more or less free from the distractions of a body in pain, I can flow with this profound part of the journey.

The broken sheets of ice are like a giant jigsaw puzzle with the pieces spread across a table. Except these jigsaw pieces have a hidden depth – when the light is just right and we pass at the right distance, we can see the turquoise depth of the ice. Sometimes we can see that it penetrates several metres below the surface of the calm water. The underwater portions taper and I think about ocean currents, water temperature, and water versus air as conductors of heat, things I know in theory, but have never seen so starkly in evidence. Now and then the flat surface is disrupted by wild ice sculptures. I wonder which might be bergy bits drifted out from their parent glaciers to mingle with the broken pack ice, and which might be fragments of pack ice, broken and buckled by storms, or flipped after their underwater centres of mass melted beyond balance.

The *Antigua* continues to slide between floes. Soon we spot a walrus, perhaps thirty metres off starboard. How did I not know that walruses are so enormous? He is magnificent. There is a dignity in his large tusks and rolls of fat; he looks well fed, and looking at him I think, "Ah, this is the life." He rests for a while on a floe and then slips into the water, swims to another floe, and climbs out. I wonder what the manoeuvre is about and whether it was inspired by our presence. I marvel at his ability to haul out on the ice with relative grace, given his mass. I study a nearby sheet and imagine myself struggling to climb out of the water.

We pass one ice floe that carries twenty large and distinct footprints indicating the straight and steady stride of a polar bear, appearing from nowhere at one edge, and walking off the other edge into nothingness. Where are the puzzle pieces that fit at each end of his path? How long since that lone bear traversed what might have been continuous kilometres across this ice?

ON SEA ICE

A few months ago, in March 2017, the National Oceanic and Atmospheric Administration (NOAA, a US government agency) measured the lowest recorded value for the maximum extent of winter Arctic sea ice area. The area covered is getting smaller and the ice is getting thinner. Multiyear ice is ice that remains frozen through at least one summer and thereby becomes thicker and more resistant to summer melt with each passing year that it survives. NOAA reports that in 2017, only 21 per cent of sea ice was multiyear ice, a stark contrast to the situation in 1985, when 45 per cent of sea ice was multiyear ice.

One of the alarmist things one hears about climate change goes something like, "The Arctic Ocean could be ice-free as early as next summer." Is it true? Well, I suppose eventually it will be that "next summer," but it isn't going to happen for a few years yet. Taking into account the large natural variability in year-to-year climate and the complex factors affecting warming and ocean currents, atmospheric scientist Alexandra Jahn and her colleagues estimated in 2016 that the first ice-free summer on the Arctic Ocean will occur between 2032 and 2058. Our only hope of delaying as long as forty years is if we aggressively reduce our greenhouse gas (GHG) emissions starting immediately.

What happens when the Arctic Ocean is ice-free in the summer? Nothing sudden. Some new shipping routes and drilling sites will open up, but all of the important changes will already be ongoing: effects on the melting of the Greenland ice sheet, release of methane from microbial activity in thawing tundra permafrost and methyl hydrates in ocean-shelf sediments, and the loss of species that depend on the summer sea ice for their survival. Nevertheless, the first year of an ice-free summer is a milestone, the timing of which is an indicator of the steepness of the rate of change between now and then (and beyond).

The loss of habitat for the walrus and many other species we haven't yet seen on this trip is already underway, as are consequent weather changes. The temperature differential between the Arctic and temperate zones drives climate forces such as the jet stream. Because Arctic temperatures are increasing at twice the rate as the global average temperature, the temperature differential is diminishing – average Arctic temperatures are already several degrees above the preindustrial baseline – with a consequent slowing and increased meandering of the jet stream. A weakened jet stream causes more dramatic and longer extreme weather such as cold spells in Europe and eastern North America, and prolonged drought such as recently suffered in California. Habitat loss and altered climate patterns don't happen all at once when the last bit of summer ice is gone. They happen in lockstep with the decline in ice. They are happening now and the rate of change is crucial. Slower change gives us more time to adapt, more time to mitigate.

EXPEDITION

It's Thursday, June 15, and we're abreast a large ice floe. Before I realize what is happening, the gangplank is down and second mate Alwin and guide Tims are on the floe. With a handheld auger they drill two holes about twenty-five metres apart. Into each hole they place a drift log salvaged from earlier landings. Ropes are cast from the *Antigua* and *voilà*! We're moored to an ice floe. Over our parkas we don life jackets and scramble down the gangplank onto the ice. Sarah's dog Nemo frolics in the snow and several of us join in. We play for a while and then board the *Antigua* for dinner. No one can stay on the ice without an armed guide on duty to watch for polar bears.

After dinner, with guides back on watchful duty, we return to the ice. This time, as with all of our other landings so far, the artists scatter and immerse themselves in their practices. Brandy is an aerial dance artist (from Toronto) and for several days she's had her ropes strung in the ship's rigging, where she'd climb up every day for a workout high over the deck. It has been beautiful to watch her go through her paces so high and graceful, framed by the ship's rigging. Now, the crew has swung a boom out over the ice floe, and from the surface of the ice Brandy is teaching others to dance in the air.

Cara hangs five feet off the ice, stretched out on her side with the rope wrapped around her waist. She has taken off her parka and is dressed in a white T-shirt, with blue jeans rolled up above the top of her boots, a grey wool beanie on her head, and binoculars around her neck. She pulls her knees up to a right angle with her hips and twists. With both hands she raises the binoculars to her eyes, scanning the horizon as she slowly spins. Cecilia is behind a tripod-mounted camera, between Cara and the ship, looking out so the backdrop to Cara is the expanse of sea ice and a sky layered in soft clouds, watercolour stripes of purple, grey, pink, and white. Cara, the surreal explorer, seeking something the rest of us can't see. I leave the small group who are waiting for a turn on the ropes and walk further out on the floe.

Anna, a Brooklyn-based multimedia artist, has spread out a small red carpet on which she is kneeling. She is waving her hands in the air and I walk a little further around to see that she is playing a theremin, an electronic musical instrument that is played without any direct contact. The theremin has two antennae, and the proximity of the musician's hand to one antenna determines pitch while the other controls volume. It is an instrument that sounds as eerie as it looks. I know this because science fiction and nerdy stuff was big in our house, and my son Jacob had a theremin. I cannot hear any sound from Anna's instrument, nor do I see cables. I wonder if she has a battery and the breeze is carrying the sound away. Or perhaps this is theatre and there is not meant to be sound.

At the other end of our floe, looking like a toddler with a pull toy, Justin, the bedhead photographer and interdisciplinary artist from Maine, walks and pulls behind him a big, bright orange plastic buoy. I walk to an edge and stand near Adam, who, with his Ansel Adams beard and camera on a tripod, is capturing video of other floes as they slowly drift past. We smile at one another, but don't say anything (through blundering, I've learned that I never know who is recording sound, so I try not to initiate conversation). Together in a Zodiac at Smeerenburgbreen, and later, back on the *Antigua*, Adam and I had discussed sublime landscapes and awe. Now, with a smile and a nod, we knew what each was experiencing here on this ice.

ON WORKING TOGETHER

Prochlorococcus is a photosynthetic, oxygen-producing, carbon dioxide–capturing bacterium the size of *E. coli*. It lives in oceans around the world and is especially abundant in warm waters, where a handful of seawater may look clear, but will contain 2.5 million *Prochlorococcus* cells. It's the most abundant photosynthetic cell on Earth.

The warm surface water of tropical and subtropical oceans doesn't mix much with the deeper cold water. At the surface there is an abundance of sunlight and carbon dioxide – the raw ingredients for photosynthesis to build sugars. Life may be sweet, but it isn't made of sugar alone. To be sure, the amino acids that make the proteins that make the molecular machines that run the cellular world, are made of sugar. Sugar and lots of nitrogen, plus some sulphur. The membranes that hold it all together for the cell are long strings of linked carbon derived from sugar, and lots of phosphate. Similarly, the nucleic acids (the A, C, T, and G of DNA) are built of sugars decorated with nitrogen and phosphate. Nitrogen, phosphate, iron, and other nutrients are essential for life, and they are in short supply in the surface waters.

At some time in the past, *Prochlorococcus* lived only in deeper water. It wasn't a bad life; there were plenty of nutrients and enough sunlight to get by. The cells grew and divided, and they were eaten by zooplankton, which in turn ... well, you already know the food-chain story. This is the story of how *Prochlorococcus* found a way to live in the nutrient-poor sunny surface waters.

The problem of living near the surface is a problem of balance – too much light relative to sparse nutrients. When a photon strikes the reaction centre of photosynthesis, it bounces an electron into a higher energy state, like a big kid bouncing a little kid on a trampoline. A chain of specialized proteins catch the little kid, I mean excited electron, and hand it from one protein to the next, breaking its fall to ever-lower energy levels. Along the way, some of the energy of the fall is captured, as though the little kid grabbed the blades of a turbine, slowing her fall and turning a wheel at the same time. The captured energy is stored in a cellular battery (a proton gradient) and is used to do all sorts of things, including form carbon–carbon bonds to build sugar from carbon dioxide, a process known as carbon fixation.

The danger of too much light is that the excess energy will damage the cell, as though it were struck by lightning – unless the excess energy is captured in a controlled way. The high-light, low-nutrient ecotype of *Prochlorococcus* has tweaked almost every part of its engine to find a balance that works. Bring on the light! Excited electrons are captured in many ways that seem futile. For example, synthesizing hydrogen peroxide soaks up some of the excess electrical energy, but hydrogen peroxide isn't useful to the cell, and worse, it can become a dangerous radical. Fortunately, because these cells are small, the hydrogen peroxide diffuses out before doing much damage.

Another way the cells cope with excess excited electrons is to capture the energy and make more sugar. While sugars are the backbone of things like amino acids and nucleic acids, without adequate nitrogen and phosphate, the cell can't use all of the sugar it makes. To avoid clogging up the works with piles of sugar, the cell secretes fixed carbon (as sugars and hydrocarbons) out into the ocean! These little cells are experts at siphoning off the excess energy arriving in the bombardment of photons. Things like the synthesis of hydrogen peroxide and secretion of fixed carbon serve as a series of safety valves. In this way, the cell avoids what would essentially be electrocution by sunshine.

On the other side of finding balance is the problem of scarce nutrients. As a side product of scrambling to keep an abundance of excited electrons under control, *Prochlorococcus* maintains a revved-up ATP supply (adenosine triphosphate, a common energy currency, used by all of life to drive cellular growth and activity), which comes in handy for the energetically costly work of scavenging for nutrients in low abundance. Although there wasn't much room to play, *Prochlorococcus* also found a few ways to build basic parts that use less nitrogen and phosphorus.

The most significant gains were made in not bothering to build certain machines at all. The core metabolism of a cell refers to the essential biochemistry required to process captured energy to make the building blocks of life: amino acids, fatty acids, and nucleotides, which are used to build proteins, lipids, and nucleic acids, respectively. *Prochlorococcus* is an impressively stripped-down, high-performance cell – they're souped-up, like my old '67 Chevy Impala.

One example is catalase, the enzyme that detoxifies hydrogen peroxide. This is an expensive machine to build because it requires not only nitrogen but also iron, often the limiting nutrient in these warm tropical waters. *Prochlorococcus* can get away with reckless pollution of its environment because other creatures sharing this environment still make this important enzyme, cleaning up the hydrogen peroxide mess, allowing *Prochlorococcus* to grow a little faster.

SAR11 is a ubiquitous and abundant oceanic bacterium. The strain of SAR11 that lives in the same waters as our high-light, low-nutrient ecotype of *Prochlorococcus* have evolved a dependency on the very sugars and hydrocarbons that are excreted by *Prochlorococcus*. In other words, just as *Prochlorococcus* has given up making catalase because others in the sea will take care of hydrogen peroxide, SAR11 has given up part of its core metabolism because as long as it shares the water with *Prochlorococcus*, the needed materials will be supplied.

Prochlorococcus invaded this new ecological space, not alone, but with a little help from its friends. Together they manage to vacuum nutrient levels down to impossibly low levels. By cooperating, they maximize total biological productivity, increase biodiversity, sequester carbon, and feed ecosystems beyond their own geographical domains. And that is the story of how a big swath of the earth's oceans that once were barren came to support life.

EXPEDITION

This morning I'm delighted to discover we spent the night moored to the ice floe, as though moored to a dock. Although we experience the ship and our floe as stationary, with other floes moving around us, the GPS tracking reveals otherwise. We drifted many kilometres in the night, our path tracking the shape of a lollipop – a loop and a stem. The top of the loop was our most northerly point of the expedition: 79°55'8"N. We arrived at the place we had been seeking when we were least aware of travelling. We didn't know we had arrived until after we were gone. We have been drifting and dreaming.

I dreamt we had left the gangplank down and a polar bear had climbed on board the *Antigua* in the night. The bear came straight to the cabin I share with M – the only unheated cabin on the ship. It seems he just wanted to stay cool. A dream triggered, perhaps, by being cold in the night. Both being outdoorsy types, M and I hadn't really paid much attention to the fact there was no heat in our cabin. The beds were cozy and we didn't spend any time in the cabin other than for sleeping. We were fine until it dawned on us that all of the other cabins were heated.

The morning sky is heavy and dark. The sea is a cold grey, rippling in an easterly wind. Being on the floe is less enchanting than yesterday. The colours are gone. I can't see below the surface of the rough water, there are no reflections, the sky is nothing but grey. It's sobering to notice the floe has undergone significant melting since yesterday – some of our footprints seem to walk right off the edge.

By afternoon, there is a hint of menace in the Arctic weather. Out for a Zodiac tour of the ice floes, we're low to the water, zipping along the edge of the sea ice. The wind is up and the water is rough. We circle close by ice sculptures that even on this gloomy grey day glow an ethereal Arctic blue so intense it seems they must be lit from inside. We explore out of sight of the ship and I grow nervous for several minutes until we loop around and the *Antigua* comes back into view.

As we make our way back to the ship, we find ourselves trapped in our little Zodiac, cornered by several floes. Again, I'm nervous. We ram and push and with a bounce we splash free. We laugh with relief and zoom towards the *Antigua*, only to discover she too is trapped in ice. We wait, unable to approach.

Pablo pulls out an apple, which he shares with the group – stranded explorers sharing the last of our rations. Beth teaches us a clapping game to help us stay warm and cheerful. It's like a symbolic game of tag. We each have a sign that defines us. For example, both hands on top of your head means Risa. We clap and sing and whoever is "it" makes the sign of another person and that person becomes "it." We are six adults of several nationalities, men and women, millennials to boomers, sitting in a tiny Zodiac floating at the edge of a sheet of sea ice that extends five hundred kilometres to the North Pole, clapping and singing and laughing. I'm enjoying the fellowship so much I'm almost sorry when Benja gets the call on his radio: the *Antigua* has successfully navigated to open water and we can now safely approach and board.

An hour and a half later, we set anchor near the fast ice of Raudfjorden. When I come out onto the deck after dinner, Eric – a tall, slim American photographer cocooned in high-tech outdoor gear that keeps him comfortable sitting still and vigilant on deck for hours at a time – has set up his tripod and has his large lens focused on a polar bear in the distance. We take turns looking and discuss what we're seeing. The bear is so far away that even with Eric's 600-millimetre lens it's hard to be certain, but the bear looks emaciated. What I see is a skinny polar bear struggling to stand and then falling down again. I'm aware the narrative of a starving polar bear is an easy one for my mind, given my obsession with climate change. I strive to see the more optimistic scenarios some of the others report – he is hunting, he is eating – but

I'm unable to align any of these with what I'm seeing through the lens. Perhaps he's very old.

This evening a few of us will give the first set of ten-minute presentations about our work. Over the next week or so, all thirty participants and the wilderness guides will share our visions, accomplishments, goals, and hopes. We crowd into the salon at the stern of the ship, under and behind the wheelhouse. Brass-railed bookshelves line the perimeter of the seating area, which is comprised of three polished wood tables, each with a curl of cushioned benches, and, in the centre of the room, chairs facing each table. The stern-most table is up a couple of steps from the other two, with chairs backing on the stairs (my least favourite spot to sit). The thirty of us "participants" are comfortably seated in the salon for meals, while the guides eat at the adjacent bar, near the buffet counters. This evening a couple of seats are given up for a screen and the guides join us at the tables. The benches are crowded and the steps are used as seats. By now we're familiar enough to be comfortable (more or less) squished together like teenagers piled on a couch to watch a movie at a sleepover. We close the shaded portholes and put dark mats over the skylight to block out the evening light.

I'm curious about the artists' projects and am excited to hear their talks. Up first is J, perhaps forty, with a pair of gold rings in one ear, a close-trimmed moustache and beard, and, although it's warm in the salon, a hand-knit wool cap pulled low over his brow and ears. He seems uneasy and says little. He uses his ten minutes to play samples from two very different compositions. In each case, I'm lost in the music and sorry when it fades out. I could have spent the evening listening to J's music. He tells us that here on the *Antigua* he is writing an Arctic-inspired string quartet.

Natalie, one of the youngest on the trip, has recently completed an undergraduate science degree in marine biology. She shows images of some of her strangely intimate life-sized paintings of sharks. We also get to see a video, shot from a drone, of a small boat at sea. In the video, Natalie is on the boat, part of a team of shark biologists at work. Suddenly a shark lunges toward the boat and the *Antigua*'s salon is filled with startled squawks and small jumps, then laughter.

Up next is Carmiel, a quiet young novelist whose brilliance I will come to appreciate in the years ahead. Like J, she says little. Carmiel reads a strangely moving story in which her protagonist, Pauline, finds a dead pelican on a winter beach and is determined to harvest its beak, "Because I used to be a zookeeper!" The language is evocative and I feel Pauline's pain. Carmiel is writing a Pauline story set in the Arctic, a story about climate change in which Pauline is being chased by a polar bear.

Next up is Brett, on the threshold of middle age, with a dark Slavic mystique. He seems nervous and races through a presentation full of ideas and projects, ongoing and completed, found music, drawings, videos, installations. I'm lost, but intrigued.

Justin tells of his residency aboard a freighter and I'm entranced by his video interviews with the crew on the trip from Portland, Maine, to Reykjavík. The videos are beautiful portraits of the eclectic souls that accompany the stuff of our lives across the seas. Justin exhibited his work from the Reykjavík trip inside a shipping container like those he escorted across the sea, but this container was strategically placed in downtown Portland, Maine. I still don't understand what he's doing with the orange buoy.

I'm up last and, after a bit of background, I tell a story of discovery in my lab. It's one of my favourites because it powerfully illustrates our evolutionary relationship with all of life. This is the story of FA2, a gene we cloned from the single-celled alga, *Chlamydomonas*. We discovered the gene in a genetic screen, searching for genes that, when mutated, lead to problems with the disassembly of cilia. A thorough comparative sequence analysis by Jeremy Parker (then a PhD student in my lab) found that while FA2 belonged to a deeply conserved gene family, it couldn't easily be aligned with any one of the dozen or so members of the family in the mammalian lineage.

Moe Mahjoub (another PhD student at the time) genetically engineered the *Chlamydomonas* FA2 gene so it would be synthesized in mammalian cells. On the end of the gene he added a sequence that encoded a fluorescent protein so if the FA2 gene were translated into protein we would be able to see it with our specially equipped microscope. Moe put the engineered gene into cultured mouse cells and we waited to see whether the mouse cells would express the algal gene, keeping in mind that the protein made would be distinct from any protein normally found in a mouse cell. Not only did the mouse cell make the protein, it delivered the protein to a highly specific and tiny spot at the base of the cilium, analogous to where we find the protein in *Chlamydomonas* cells. When I show the photomicrograph of the highly localized algal protein in the mouse cell, Cara gasps, "Wow!" I smile. That is precisely how I felt when Moe first showed me that particular result.

I tell how we went on to collaborate with a human geneticist and discovered that mutations in a related gene in humans caused a rare and severe form of polycystic kidney disease in children. By expressing genes with the human mutations in mouse cells, we were able to show that localization to the cilia was essential for normal function of this gene.

After all of these years, I'm still stunned I got to do this amazing work probing the machines of life. It's fun to share the stories and inspire a little awe for molecules. And yet, my feelings about the positive response in the room aren't so pure as that. I can sense I've impressed this group with my accomplishments and that feels nice. But also, it doesn't. In these situations, I struggle with a sensitivity about expectations. I sense that some people are impressed because they are surprised and I am annoyed that they are surprised. Why shouldn't I, an older woman, have done these things?

When I was thirteen, I was flummoxed when my little brother got to hike the West Coast Trail with the Boy Scouts, while in Canadian Girls in Training (CGIT) I was learning how to neatly fold and tuck the corners of a bed sheet (this was before fitted sheets). Seven days of backpacking on an old life-saving trail along the rugged west coast of Vancouver Island – it was my dream. I must have been intolerable because the next summer my father took me on the hike. We slept on the beach under a tarp and cooked on a campfire. One of my many memories from that trip is sitting on a log watching the sunset over the ocean, Dad and I each with our own fork, passing a can of baked beans back and forth between us.

Gender issues are a little like global warming and weather. The changes seem small – a one degree Celsius change in average global temperature – and the impacts can seem remote – devastating sea level rise sometime in the future, droughts and famine on the other side of the earth. It can be hard to connect the dots, and hard to care. I was socialized to accept gender bias at the same time as the cultural milieu around me was changing. I was a feminist unaware of how deeply I'd internalized the messages of inferiority. We know climate change is happening, but we don't feel it. We don't feel all of those little changes adding up, until we do.

In my youth, I was frustrated, but accepting. As an undergraduate I was told only male students could go on the research trip to the Serengeti.

I was advised not to major in my favourite subject because there were no jobs for women with degrees in math. At a gathering for tea one afternoon in 1980, when I was a graduate student in oceanography, there was a lively discussion of the lack of academic jobs and whether professors should perhaps not be taking on so many graduate students. My thesis advisor piped up and said, "Why do you think I take on so many women students? It's because after grad school they get married and have babies and I don't need to worry about finding them jobs."

Eventually, curiosity about how life works at a molecular level drove me to get my PhD in biochemistry and genetics at the University of Connecticut in Storrs. ("You're the smartest woman I've ever met," said Tom, a classmate. I wanted to know if that meant I was almost as smart as him.) As a PhD student, I attended a lecture with my son sleeping peacefully against my chest in his hand-me-down green corduroy snuggly. At the end of the talk, I asked a question. Unfortunately, the speaker, Nobel laureate Ilya Prigogine, dismissed it as not a good question. Prigogine had seen me not as a serious scientist, but as a woman with a baby.

I went on to postdoctoral studies in Dallas, Texas, with a man who won the Nobel Prize two years after I was in his lab. I had interviewed with Alfred Gilman at a conference, talking excitedly about new developments in the field. Scoring a position in the Gilman Lab was a coup. Sadly, when I arrived in Dallas with my then husband and three-year-old son, I quickly learned I had made the wrong choice. In formal lab meetings, my ideas weren't acknowledged, yet when a male colleague raised the same point later in the meeting, Al would praise him for his brilliance. This and other small slights led me to wonder why he had ever accepted me – he really didn't seem to like me. Finally, one of the senior members of the lab revealed that Al was angry when I arrived with a child. Apparently, he'd said something like, "Women can be successful scientists or they can be successful mothers. They cannot be both." I found another lab to complete my postdoctoral studies, and then after another year, landed a faculty position in the Department of Cell Biology at Emory University in Atlanta.

To attribute any specific instance of perceived bias to gender was akin to claiming that global warming exacerbated the damage of a specific hurricane. Women who spoke up didn't have the right stuff; they were crying "male chauvinism" instead of acknowledging their own shortcomings. I could not afford to be one of those women. It was worse than that. For years I didn't believe I had been affected. I believed that I had persevered and overcome. Now, as I see the threat of climate change on the horizon, I finally understand the depth of wounds inflicted by gender bias and misogyny.

Triggered by the #MeToo movement, I recently spent an entire hour venting and raging to my therapist about the misogyny I've experienced. In spite of his assurances that my anger and frustration were appropriate to the circumstances, I felt dirty afterwards. I felt as though I'd been making excuses for my own failings. Like the damage left in the aftermath of a global warming–charged superstorm, the shaken confidence and washed-out opportunities have taken their toll on me.

I suppress my negative reaction to some of the positive responses from the group and continue with photos of watermelon snow and micrographs of snow algae from the mountains around my lab in Burnaby. I don't yet have a scientific story of my own to tell about these algae, so I lay out the questions we'll be asking.

It can't be easy for microbes to live on the surface of snow. How do snow algae colonize the snow afresh each spring? What interactions with bacteria, archaea, fungi, and various microscopic eukaryotes and viruses allow this community to thrive on the snow, where biochemistry is slow and the light is bright? The snow algae must be the primary producers – capturing energy from the sun and converting it to chemical energy, reducing carbon dioxide and linking the carbons together to form sugars. Do they, like *Prochlorococcus*, spit out sugars that feed other microbes? Do bacteria and fungi provide clean-up services or perhaps vitamins? We know this community often produces mucus, presumably to prevent dehydration in this strange desert. Does the mucus also serve to hold the community together, keeping the microbes from being washed away? I'm curious about the viruses. Have they made peace with some of the key bacteria and do they help defend the community from intruding microbes? Do the different species communicate across kingdoms?

I know from hours at the microscope in my lab spent looking at samples of snow algae from our local mountains that these assemblages of microscopic snow creatures are beautiful. The algae glow like jewels – translucent spring-green spheres; round rubies set in a translucent ridged wall; oblong green, red, or orange cells that look like autumn leaves; larger, fat, juicy orange cells, some with four cilia that protrude from a single tunnel in a thick cell wall. There is an unexplored diversity of ciliates and rotifers and the occasional too-cute tardigrade with its belly full of red cells. And then there are the fungi. One common fungus has three arms growing out of a central cytoplasm. Another attaches to the algal cells and inserts hyphae through the algal cell wall. Are they sipping on the fatty red pigment, like a child drinking strawberry soda through a straw?

Samples from mountain meadows look different from samples collected from snow banks in the forest, which, in turn, are comprised of different assemblages of cells than samples collected in the rocky high alpine. My graduate students and I want to understand what drives the formation of these different communities. Here in the Arctic, the snow environments are unlike anything in the alpine – twenty-four hours of daylight, for one thing. I've brought along a microscope with excellent optics and I'm curious to see living communities of Arctic snow algae.

In a conspiratorial tone, I briefly explain the chronology of applying for a spot on this expedition before discovering snow algae in my own backyard. Everyone laughs as I come clean about the proposed Arctic snow algae project being my ticket for this trip. They resonate with my deeper reasons for being here: the art and science of climate change. I briefly mention my activism with the backdrop of a photo of me in handcuffs. Henceforth, I am good-naturedly teased for being a badass.

ACTIVIST

In 2008, I was standing at the front of a large, well-appointed lecture hall at the Max Planck Institute of Molecular Cell Biology and Genetics in Dresden, Germany. I was delivering a lecture on my lab's research to the scientists who work at this important hub of cell biology. I'd been nervous for months, but once I began my talk, all of that fell away and I was in the flow of the science. That feeling lasted for about forty minutes, which is when I looked at the clock and realized I'd made the rookie mistake of trying to cover too much material. I was going to have to edit on the fly to arrive at the ending of my story by the appointed time. I rushed through the material and in the final ten minutes I managed to confuse and lose an audience that had been hanging on every word. I felt like I'd blown my big moment, but as soon as the questions began, I knew that it was not so bad.

What I didn't know at the time was that I would look back on Dresden as a turning point. The trip happened during what were, in retrospect, my peak years as a cell biologist. My visit to the Max Planck was a celebration of that, but coincidentally, the visit to Dresden also played a role in pulling my focus away from cells.

For two days, I was immersed in intimate and intense discussions about such things as whether the cilia of neurons were releasing vesicles into the cerebral spinal fluid, and, if so, were they signalling to distant cells in this way? And, do the touch-sensitive bristles of fruit flies use a protein related to one my group had discovered to transduce physical sensations into neuronal signals? Such fun!

When my visit to the Institute was over, I had a day in Dresden. My host, Joe Howard, took me to the Gemäldegalerie Alte Meister. We walked past masterpiece after masterpiece, slowly, but not stopping. When we arrived at what was obviously Joe's destination, we stood for a long time looking at Vermeer's *Girl Reading a Letter at an Open Window*. I was captivated by the hyper-reality of Vermeer's light.

It was a Saturday, and after the museum we joined Joe's family at the winter market. Later, I went on my own to the German Hygiene Museum. A science museum may seem like a strange choice in this city with so much history and art – especially after two days of intense cell biology – but the science museum was holding a special exhibit on climate change.

I had seen graphs of atmospheric carbon dioxide concentration over time before, but this exhibit used an entire wall to present the superimposed plots of temperature and carbon dioxide for the past 400,000 years. Writing this, I smile at my geeky scientist self – to feel whole-body immersion in a graph was a cool experience. I walked the timeline along the jagged bounce of several glacial–interglacial oscillations: carbon dioxide levels during interglacial periods were at eye level (around 300 ppm); during glacial periods carbon dioxide was down around my knees (180 to 200 ppm). Up and down I bounced, following the trace that vaguely resembled a heartbeat. When I arrived at the Holocene, the 10,000-year-long interglacial period of climate stability during which human civilization developed, carbon dioxide levels were again at eye level, until, just about when the heart beat would have had me dipping down, the trace shot abruptly toward the ceiling, higher than I could reach. It was an almost vertical line because the time was so short and the increase in carbon dioxide substantial – almost as much of an increase above the Holocene as the Holocene was above ice-age levels.

For two days I had been in constant conversation with brilliant scientists at the Max Planck. Not once did any of us mention the data that would soon be impacting our lives most profoundly. To be fair, the topic of global warming had come up with Joe's family, and it was his daughter who had directed me to this exhibit. Still, I was hit hard by the awareness that, for the most part, my science colleagues back home and around the globe weren't talking about global warming. I didn't understand this and it left me doubting my own fears about the data. Was I overreacting? If I understood the data correctly, I needed to be devoting myself to this important problem.

EXPEDITION

After the ten-minute talks in the salon, some of us are gathered around the bar when Brett pokes his head in and encourages us to come out on deck. Down in her cabin, listening through the hull of the ship, Natalie had heard the sound of seals singing. Rachael quickly connected her submerged hydrophone to a speaker she brought along for sharing sonic experiences. It's such a gift to be together on deck experiencing the seal song in real time! The song begins with a rapid rise in pitch, followed by a slower cascading drop, and then suddenly rises again and slowly cascades to lower tones, until there's another sudden rise, which cascades again, this time for longer, going lower. Then there is silence – until, unexpectedly, the song starts again. I exclaim repeatedly in wonder as we are serenaded by *Erignathus barbatus*, the bearded seal. Like some human-made music, the song, though mournful to my ear, fills me with joy. We grin at one another and laugh every time we are surprised by the initiation of a new round of the song.

I stand on the deck of the *Antigua* with this amazing group of people, surrounded by sea ice, mountains, and two glaciers flowing to the sea. On the foredeck, Eric has turned his lens on another distant polar bear; the one I had watched walk across the fast ice is now fast asleep. It's a little past midnight and light as day. Time for me to get some sleep.

By morning, I am sick. My throat is sore and my sinuses are painful. The cold that has been making its rounds on the ship has caught up with me. We're anchored at Ytre Norskøya, near the northern tip of Spitsbergen, and I'm sorry to miss the morning landing and hikes. Justin has also stayed behind. He asks me, "Is your microscope powerful enough to see blood cells?"

"Yes, it certainly is," I reply. "Although, without stains, we will probably only see red cells. Maybe if we are lucky we'll find a few white cells, but we won't be able to see any of their features."

We set up the microscope and his camera clicks into the adaptor. Justin pokes his finger with a needle and squeezes a drop of blood onto a microscope slide. I learn that he is keen to look at his own blood and capture some microscopic video because blood has been an ever-present focus in his life – Justin has haemophilia. I explain that his blood cells will look just like anybody's blood cells. He already knows that, but still there is something special about seeing his own blood.

When I was a kid and first learned about cells and blood, I was fascinated by the idea that cells are the fundamental unit of life, each cell a living thing in its own right. I remember one day out playing in the forest next to our house. I don't remember how I got the scratch – climbing a tree or building a tree fort – but I remember sitting in the dirt with blood seeping from a scratch on my arm. I was feeling bad, not because it hurt, but because I was thinking of all of those blood cells leaking from my body and dying on my skin. That I would one day become a biologist who studied cells was beyond anything I could have possibly imagined.

Justin is thrilled. He exclaims when the cells suddenly flow in response to a little pressure from my finger on the coverslip. He watches the cells flow one way and then another, chattering about the flow of bergy bits and the shapes of cells. He is free-associating possible uses of the video for an art project. To me these biconcave homogeneous red cells are about as bland as cell microscopy gets. I dream of blowing Justin's mind when we find snow algae to put under the microscope.

Three others are spending the morning in the salon. At the other lower table, J is once again lost in thought writing music on a large pad of manuscript paper. Hailey is editing photos on her laptop. At the upper aft table, Jesus is painting. The three tables in the salon are the only places to spread out for microscopy, painting, editing photos, composing music, writing, and all of the various things that happen between meals. Now, we must pack up and clear off the tables because the adventurers are returning from their hike; it's almost lunchtime.

I partially disassemble the microscope and pack it away in its case. I tuck the case under the buffet table and slip downstairs to wash up and have a few horizontal moments on my bunk before lunch. When I return to the salon, I line up behind Carleen. "Look," she says, "fresh salad again. How do they do it?" J joins the line behind me and expresses his hope that the marzipan dessert we all enjoyed a few days ago will make another appearance. (It never does.)

By the time lunch is over, the clouds have settled around us and it's snowing heavily. We spend the afternoon on the *Antigua*, slowly making our way south along the coast, scanning for wildlife. After a couple of hours, we arrive back in Fuglefjorden, a bay we visited on our way north. It's snowing more lightly now. Although the Arctic winter was warm and the winter sea ice thinner and less extensive than it has historically been, spring has been cold. I wonder if this explains the surprising absence of snow algae. Perhaps when we return to the southern regions of Spitsbergen we'll find some patches of red snow.

We continue south, the clouds lift, and we're treated to some glorious sunny warmth, and spectacular views of the coastline. We travel through the night that is day.

ON THE KEELING CURVE

I looked up atmospheric carbon dioxide levels a few days before boarding the *Antigua*: on 6 June 2017, the daily average was 410 ppm. In 1958, David Charles Keeling began monitoring atmospheric carbon dioxide levels at the Mauna Loa Observatory on Hawaii. He observed daily and seasonal fluctuations, and a steady rise in levels, year over year. When the measurements began, carbon dioxide levels were around 315 ppm. (When I was in Dresden in 2008, carbon dioxide was about 385 ppm.) The pre-1958 data I had seen on the wall of the Hygiene Museum were obtained by measuring concentrations of carbon dioxide in air bubbles frozen in ice cores from the Arctic and Antarctica. The real-time data being measured at Mauna Loa (and now at many other stations around the globe) are (so far) freely available online.

In the decade after my experience at the Hygiene Museum, I wondered many times about how bright and knowledgeable people, people who understood the science of climate change and knew the facts about causes and impending impacts, could continue on as if the world was as it had been. I can't do it. Once I understood the situation, I had to give my all to the project of shifting our trajectory.

Today we're living in a world that is, on average, one degree Celsius warmer than it was in pre-industrial times. Almost forty years ago, James Hansen and his colleagues reported a global mean temperature rise of 0.4 degrees Celsius over the one hundred years from 1880 to 1979. Although this temperature increase was small and difficult to pick out from variation due to volcanic eruptions, the brightness of the sun, and other drivers of global mean temperature, the team was able to calculate that the temperature increase was in line with predictions based on the known warming properties of greenhouse gases accumulating in the atmosphere.

Based on these data, Hansen and his team made testable predictions. A decade later, the team was able to show the accuracy of their earlier predictions. These are landmark papers, yet at the time some scientists criticized Hansen, claiming he was sensationalizing his results to attract more attention and funding.

In a more recent paper, "Ice Melt, Sea Level Rise and Superstorms" (2016), Hansen and his co-authors present a peer-reviewed prediction that, given business-as-usual fossil fuel emissions, we can expect to see multi-metre sea level rise within 50 to 150 years. Hansen is a rigorous scientist with an exceptional track record of careful analysis. This particular result has enormous policy implications because that level of sea level rise would flood every coastal city in the world. Yet, here in Canada, where I live in a major coastal city, we're extracting fossil fuels from the ground like there is no tomorrow. Is Hansen's result in doubt?

Even without being an expert in the field, it's easy to ballpark expectations. We know the global temperature today matches the peak temperature during the Eemian, the last interglacial period, approximately 120,000 years ago, when our ancestors were trading shells and mixing it up with Neanderthals. The geological record shows that there is always a time lag between a temperature increase and sea level rise. Sea level in the Eemian was six to nine metres higher than it is today. So, to start, we know we're already locked in for multi-metre sea level rise. The question is, how fast will it happen?

The *rate* of sea level rise depends on the temperature driving the melting of ice sheets. Global average temperatures today are continuing to rise (above Eemian levels) and the rate of increase is creeping past linear and into exponential. This rapid temperature rise is being driven by carbon dioxide levels that are already far above Eemian levels. Hansen and his colleagues used data relating past carbon dioxide levels to the rates of sea level rise and applied those parameters to our current levels of carbon dioxide and rates of GHG emissions.

The result of this calculation is that we will have multi-metre sea level rise in 50 to 150 years. Importantly, the climate scientists who provided peer review of the "Ice Melt" paper or subsequent commentary – checking assumptions and calculations – do not question that without serious and rapid action to alter the trajectory, multi-metre sea level rise will happen with the rapidity predicted by Hansen and his team. This conclusion is not in doubt.

I think of the six of us in that little Zodiac, momentarily trapped in the sea ice and then prevented from returning to the *Antigua* because she too was trapped in ice. I think not of our vulnerability, but rather of the warm fellowship. Our survival depended on getting safely back on board the *Antigua* and everyone did their part to make that happen – the captain and crew navigating the *Antigua* out of the ice, and those of us stranded in the Zodiac clapping and singing to stay warm and calm.

In their 2017 paper, "Young People's Burden," Hansen and his team conclude, "continued high fossil fuel emissions unarguably sentences young people to either a massive, implausible clean-up or growing deleterious climate impacts or both." This is a more dramatic statement than what we're hearing from the IPCC. Why? Because Hansen doesn't hedge his results with, for example, carbon capture technologies that aren't yet feasible. I'm grateful to Hansen – just tell it to me straight.

Also in 2017, in a paper titled "A Roadmap for Rapid Decarbonization," Johan Rockström, Hans Joachim Schellnhuber, and their colleagues calculate that to have a middling (66 per cent) chance of meeting the Paris target of staying below a two degree Celsius rise in temperature, we need to stop increasing GHG emissions by 2020, and then cut emissions by 50 per cent every decade. If negative emissions come on line, our odds of avoiding two degrees Celsius will improve, but even a two degree Celsius warming will drive a rapid and dangerous rise in sea level.

ACTIVIST

It was a gorgeous spring day and I longed to be out in the sunshine walking the seawall or hiking in the woods. I pulled my attention back to the computer screen and the report I was writing. I was bored. Soon I was checking my email. Ah! A message had arrived in the five minutes since the last time I checked. It was from my friend Alejandro.

Alejandro, a professional ecologist, was considering joining an action and was wondering if I might be interested. He sent along a newsletter from James Hansen (the same) containing a letter addressed to Warren Buffett (billionaire, philanthropist, and owner of Burlington Northern Santa Fe railroad, the BNSF) from a group called Stop Coal! The letter gave Buffett one week's notice that the group would spend twenty-four hours preventing BNSF coal trains from passing through White Rock, British Columbia, to deliver coal to Vancouver ports for export to Asia. The group had chosen May 5 to join the International Day of Action organized by 350.org with the theme of "Connecting the Dots." As the group said, "We cannot think of a more important connection to emphasize than the one between burning coal and putting our collective future at risk."

This was April 2012 and I was primed for more radical climate activism. After returning from Dresden, I continued to believe governments would soon act with appropriate regulations, a carbon tax, reduced subsides for fossil fuels, and more. I wrote letters to politicians, attended rallies, and focused on reducing my carbon footprint by eating only a little meat, flying less, buying things second hand or not at all, and taking transit instead of driving. I also talked a lot about this stuff. I even inspired a few friends. But I knew that things were not changing fast enough.

Alejandro and I didn't know who was behind Stop Coal! and neither of us had ever been involved in civil disobedience before, but we were both feeling a strong drive to do whatever we could to help push society toward turning the corner on averting the looming changes in our climate. We'd both upped our game with personal lifestyle changes and with political noisemaking, but these actions were beginning to feel inadequate.

White Rock is a small oceanside community about sixty kilometres south from where I live. We had six days to prepare. We learned about civil disobedience and our rights in British Columbia, we learned first aid for tear gas, and we plotted our public transit route to the site. We filled our water bottles and packed extra bandanas and granola bars – and, in my pack, a few CIHR grant proposals to read. Although the action was on a Sunday, I was serving on a peer review panel and I had a deadline approaching.

The morning was chilly and wet when Alejandro and I boarded the first bus of our trip. By the time we arrived at the railway tracks, after two hours on transit and a walk of several blocks, the clouds were breaking and the sun was out. The site that we'd been directed to was near the White Rock Pier, a popular local beach where the train tracks ran along the shore. About thirty people were gathered on the wide public steps near where a major beach access point crossed the tracks. Protestors mingled with locals out to enjoy a warm spring day.

Alejandro and I wanted to know what was happening. At first, we didn't recognize anyone and no one knew who we were. No one wanted to answer our questions. Those who'd organized the action were cautious about letting us know they were associated with the protest and even more cautious about letting us know their names. Safely stopping a coal train is not a trivial undertaking, and, as we later learned, this action had been two years in the planning. Eventually, people we knew in common arrived and vouched for us – we were not moles for the RCMP or the train company.

It was a long day of cat-and-mouse, three-way negotiations between us, the RCMP, and BNSF. BNSF very much wanted to get a train through on that day and we were determined to stop it. We knew from our spotters on the other side of the border that BNSF was holding the train a few miles down the track. They tried to wait us out. Eventually the media gave up and went home. We stayed. The police stayed. The big, burly, physically intimidating BNSF security team stayed.

As we waited for the train to come, I sat on the tracks and read scientific research proposals. The early morning had been rainy, but the day was sunny and warm – lots of locals were out to spend time at the beach, crossing the tracks near us. As I looked up from a grant application, a young man made eye contact with me and spat out, "Get a job." Another shouted, "You hypocrites! You all drove your SUVs here."

Finally, BNSF brought the train down the tracks. I knew it would stop. I knew this was theatre. Yet the train kept coming. It was a big train and slow to stop; it approached much closer than I would have thought safe. As the engine loomed my bowels churned and then they churned some more as I remembered I was about to be arrested. It wasn't until I was in handcuffs and being escorted to a police car while the others were taken to a patrol wagon that I realized I was the only woman arrested and would likely go to a cell by myself. Churn.

My emotions were a strange cocktail of fear, shame, and euphoria. Part of me was proud that with this bold action I would join the ranks of those who had courageously stood up for the right and the good. Unfortunately, I didn't enjoy the moment because fear and shame kicked the euphoria down. Some in the crowd were jeering as we were arrested, and instead of standing tall and smiling, I hung my head. Just before I was put in the back of the police car, a woman broke from the crowd of onlookers. She was crying and the policeman who was escorting me allowed her to approach; she gave me a hug and whispered, "Thank you, thank you." The tension drained from my body with the realization someone understood what was happening.

1. Arthur Bird in front of his cabin, 120 miles from Cameron Bay, Great Bear Lake, circa 1933.
Photographer unknown.

2A. Top: *Antigua* at anchor with Smeerenburgbreen in the distance.
2B. Bottom: Afternoon landing near Fjortende Julibreen.

3A. Top: Smeerenburgbreen calving.
3B. Bottom: Zodiac tour of Smeerenburgbreen (author at far left).

Photographs by Hailey Lane.

4A. Top: Morning landing in front of Recherchebreen. Photograph by Justin Levesque.
4B. Bottom: Polar bear on the western shore near Fridtjofbreen. Photograph by Hailey Lane.

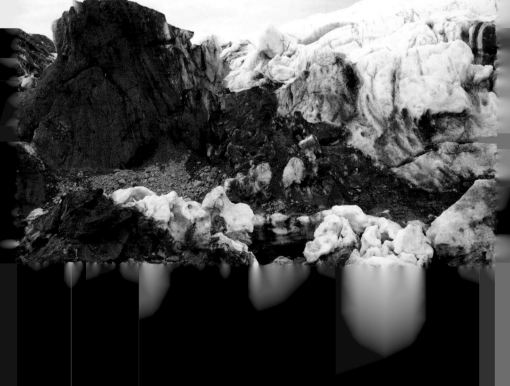

6A. Top: Sarah Gerats preparing to unfurl sails.
6B. Bottom: Ice.

Photographs by Hailey Lane.

7A. Top: Bergy bit.
7B. Bottom: Edge of Arctic sea ice.

Photographs by the author.

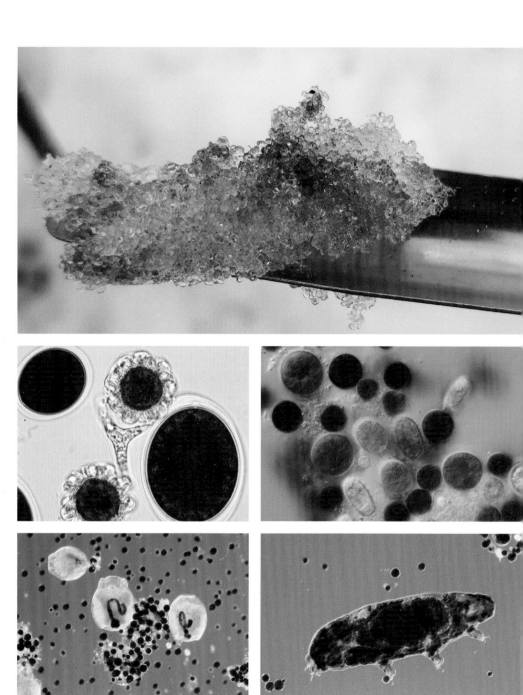

8A. Top: Stainless steel spatula with scoop of watermelon snow.

8B and 8C. Middle: Photomicrographs of field samples from two different snow algae blooms.

8D and 8E. Bottom: Rotifers (left) and a tardigrade (right) are among
the many organisms found in watermelon snow.

Photographs by Quarmby Lab PhD student Casey Engstrom.

EXPEDITION

It's Sunday morning and we have set anchor at Blomstrandhamna. The water is flat and free of ice; low mountains and expansive glaciers surround us. The view from the ship is exhilarating and I take lots of photos. Unfortunately, I slept poorly last night and I'm feeling miserable today, sneezing and blowing my nose like crazy. I miss the morning landing. In the salon, Hailey helps me with some photo editing and we spend some time on the microscope. Hailey is keen to film her own blood. We set up her camera on the microscope. She quickly learns how to tweak the settings on the microscope and the computer that we've connected to her camera. She is exclaiming at everything she sees. I smile. Artists, I think, are not so different from scientists.

Bee, a young printmaker and illustrator from the UK, returns from the morning trip with some samples from the landing. After lunch I am still feeling low and not much in the mood to go to the trouble of setting up the microscope again. I am also tired of spending so much time in the salon. But Bee is excited, so I rally. "Sure! Let's do it! Let's see what you have in those samples." One of Bee's projects is to write and illustrate a children's book documenting her Arctic adventure. For the next hour, I'm part of Bee's adventure. I show her how to use the pipet to transfer some of her sample to a microscope slide and set her up to look at the sample. We see nothing but bits of dirt. I'm not surprised because Bee has collected mud from the foot of the glacier, cold glacial meltwater mixed with bits of ground-up rock that has been frozen for millennia. I don't expect to see it teeming with life. But Bee is terribly disappointed, so we try a little harder.

I tell Bee that when the abundance of cells is low, we're unlikely to see anything interesting in one small drop. To improve our odds, we concentrate the sample. I instruct Bee and she transfers one millilitre of her sample to a smaller tube, one that fits into the bubble microfuge (a centrifuge so small it can be held in one hand). We turn on the microfuge, the sample whirls, and grains of sand and microorganisms alike are all concentrated in the bottom of the tube. Bee uses the pipet to transfer a drop from the bottom of this tube to a fresh microscope slide. She puts her eyes to the microscope and takes a minute to focus. "I saw something! Something just swam by!" Whatever it was has disappeared from her field of view and Bee is having trouble finding it again. I take a turn at the microscope and scan the slide. Bee's creature turns out to be a gorgeous, bright-green algal cell, similar to my beloved *Chlamydomonas*. Bee is delighted. I'm thrilled. This never gets old.

Back in my unheated cabin, I seek quiet and rest. I decide a shower would be a great way to warm up and perhaps feel a little better. I recall the captain's words during orientation. I understand water conservation and I know how to take a short shower. But in this case, I'm cold and sick and living in the only unheated cabin on the ship. And I haven't showered for several days. I luxuriate in a ten-minute shower. And then I throw open the door to let the steamy heat warm our cold cabin. The fire alarm goes off while I stand naked and dripping. I dry as quickly as I can, pull on my long wool underwear, some pants, a sweater, and then socks, boots, jacket, and hat. I grab my life jacket and hurry up the steep stairs. Of course, I'm the last one on deck. The captain patiently waits for me to find my place in line (wet hair peeking out under my hat) before he begins my public reprimand. I dare not make eye contact with any of the other participants for fear of offending the captain further with a giggle.

Late afternoon, while many of the others are off on a hike, I stand on the foredeck appreciating the amazing fact of being here. That is when the deckhand, Ludo – tall and broad, with grizzled, salt-and-pepper hair and beard, twinkling, bright blue eyes, a boyish grin, and the easy bearing of one who is living the good life and knows it – brings me an unanticipated hot lemon and ginger with honey. The real thing, fresh-squeezed lemon juice and diced chunks of fresh ginger root. It is perfect.

After a good sleep, I'm feeling great this morning. It cheers me to see we're still anchored in front of Blomstrandbreen. I'm determined not to miss any of today's opportunities to visit shore.

Our expedition leader, Sarah, has been exploring Svalbard for a decade. She visited Blomstrandbreen when the island in front of the glacier was still known as Blomstrndhalvoya – "Flower Beach Peninsula." Blomstrandbreen is retreating so rapidly that in less than a decade the peninsula has been revealed as an island. Susan, a Canadian photographer, told me that yesterday's landing elicited some deep emotions for her. Susan is an artist around my age with a strong activist background. She teaches social practice and photography at Emily Carr University of Art and Design in Vancouver and in six months I'll be doing a presentation with her, sharing climate science and our experience of the Arctic. Susan describes how on yesterday's landing she hiked off a short distance on her own and stood staring at a mountain that looked like it was weeping. She described the mountains at this site as naked and slumping. "They shouldn't be like this. They should be dressed in snow and standing tall and firm." As I listened to her words, it sounded like she was describing the experience of visiting a beloved elderly relative in a care home, bereft of former dignity.

We land on a beach close to the glacier and it's immediately apparent how this place embodies the melting of the Arctic. The dominant sound is running water; the dominant colour is brown. Dirty streams in full flood form a small delta of braided mud that I find impossible to walk across for fear of getting stuck or, at the least, losing a boot. Small waterfalls seep from layers of ice and mud with uplifts and undulations reminiscent of rock formations. Here the patchy snow is soft and wet, good conditions for snow algae. Aside from a false alarm when Carmiel finds red snow that turns out to be some sort of excrement, the snow is white or muddy. I try to find my way around the mud to where Robert – one of the other Canadians, an installation and media artist – is branding the glacier with the word "Mine." But I can't find a way through the mud. I turn instead and climb a scree slope for the views. This place looks lifeless, but then I remember Bee's green algal cell from yesterday. I look around at the dirty water and mud – glacial silt being released after being ground from bedrock, frozen for millennia. Where did that little green guy come from?

I think of the old ideas of spontaneous generation, maggots from rotting meat, algae from mud. Perhaps our solitary algal cell hatched from a long-frozen spore; perhaps it blew in on the wind or was washed down from the surface of the glacier. We know better than to think the algal cell arose spontaneously from the mud – watching it under the microscope we saw the distinctive green of modern single-celled algae with their chlorophyll-based photosynthesis. And it was swimming! This was no newcomer to the living world. This cell was clearly the product of a long and distinguished evolutionary lineage.

ON COOPERATION

Lacking any physical evidence of how life originated and with only a vague idea of the conditions on Earth about four billion years ago, studying the origin of life is a difficult thing to do. Nevertheless, it's an active field of research and that tickles me. What could be more central to understanding our place in the cosmos than knowing about our deep roots, the very origin of life?

Living things grow and replicate; they make copies of themselves. Since the discovery of DNA, its structure and code, origin of life research has focused primarily on the information aspect of life – how did early life make copies of itself? The oldest and simplest form of molecular replication is complementary copying RNA (a simpler relative of DNA). It has been assumed chemical conditions on early Earth were sufficient to drive the formation of the original RNA. RNA is a single-stranded chain of nucleotides. Like proteins, RNA molecules fold into three-dimensional shapes that are entirely dependent upon the linear sequence of subunits. These various shapes can form binding pockets that other molecules fit into; the polymers can thereby serve as catalysts, or enzymes, favouring particular reactions.

Occasionally a particular RNA will have a sequence that dictates folding into a shape that happens to bind to another RNA strand and use that sequence as a template to assemble a complementary strand, a bit like building a mirror image. That is, some specific sequences of RNA fold into little copying machines, making complementary copies of every

RNA strand they happen to grab. This activity was predicted by theory and then proven possible by laboratory experiments.

A second round of copying, in which the machine copies the copy, will reproduce the original sequence. When a copying machine copies another copying machine, then every other copy will also be a copying machine. Voila! Replication is accomplished.

For RNA replication to happen with enough frequency for it to get traction, we need a way to keep the strands in proximity to one another; we need compartmentalization. Another important problem that must be solved is provision of a consistent flux of energy. But for now, it is enough to pause and appreciate what this feat of RNA is telling us about our origins.

This is original cooperation: While a long RNA molecule is able to make mirror image copies of any RNA it encounters, we only get replication when this RNA pairs up with a partner, another strand of RNA with similar prowess. Only with the back-and-forth of original–complement–new copy of original–new complement, and so on, will the team produce an abundance of new copying machines – raw material for evolution.

From our early days as molecules, through the entire four billion years of our evolution, survival has hung on various bits working together – molecules with molecules, cells with cells, individuals with individuals. Cooperation is integral to our continuance. This is acutely true today as human civilization faces complex problems, climate change being but one.

Complex problems arise from systems that are a nasty mess of hetero-geneity, stochastic events, dynamic interactions, interdependent variables, nonlinear relationships, and feedback loop-de-loops. Complex problems do not have "a solution." Rather, navigating complex problems requires agreement on preferred outcomes and cooperative efforts in the direction of those outcomes. Context and perspective are important and diverse segments of society need to participate in working towards the goals. Just as no one molecule can be the seed of life, no individual (or small group of like-minded individuals) can be expected to "solve" a problem like climate change. And yet, in our current political systems in Canada, the US, the UK, and elsewhere, we place power in the hands of small, homogeneous groups. In majority governments, there is no cooperation.

ON POLITICAL REPRESENTATION

I don't have much of an appetite for electoral politics. Yet in 2015, I jumped into the metaphorical deep end by becoming a candidate in the Canadian federal election. I was in a state of panic about the climate and believed I could be one of those much-needed voices in Parliament pushing hard for meaningful climate action. Sometimes, being naïve helps us question things we might otherwise accept. Perhaps my candidacy was one of those times.

In 2015, the Canadian Parliament expanded from 308 to 338 seats. I ran as the Green candidate in one of the new ridings (districts), Burnaby North–Seymour. Because it was a new riding, there was no incumbent candidate. The field was open and a 24 August headline in the local press, the *Tyee*, read, "Burnaby North–Seymour: Canada's Perilously Tight Four-Way Race: We should take this new riding seriously; all four parties certainly have." I was running to win.

I have many strong memories from those ten months. I remember one beautiful June evening, when the sun was still shining as we started our after-dinner canvass of a neighbourhood not too far from the campaign office. The house we approached was typical for the neighbourhood: a small, white stucco rancher, built in the 1960s or 1970s, with a patchy front lawn bisected by a concrete walk that ended with four steps up to the front door. As I introduced myself to a woman on the doorstep, she began closing the door on me.

"Not interested," she said.

"Wait!" I pleaded. "Please tell me why you don't want to talk to me." I had learned that people might not want to hear what I had to say, but they were almost always willing to tell me what was on their mind. As she opened the door again, I watched her mood transition from anger to despair, perhaps matching the despair she'd heard in my voice.

"I like you," she said. "But I don't think you have a chance, so I am going to vote for the NDP because they can win."

"But if people like you vote for me," I said, "I will have a chance to win!"

She started to close the door again.

"I'm sorry," I said. "I don't want to argue. I want to listen. Why do you think I can't win?"

She stood with the door ajar, her hand on the knob ready to complete the action of closing. "Because the NDP were here yesterday and told me they could win a majority of seats and form government. The Greens have no hope of forming government, so if I vote for you I am wasting my vote. The NDP candidate stands for all the same things that you do, but she will be able to actually get things done. If I vote for you, Carol Baird – is that her name? – might not get enough votes to beat the Conservative. I don't want Harper to get in. I like you but I am not going to vote for you and risk helping Harper. Now I have to go." She stepped back and readied to close the door.

"Thank you for sharing that with me."

"Thank you for your climate work. Please don't split the vote. Don't let Harper win." Click. Of course, I would not be running if the NDP stood for all the same things as the Greens. The NDP was, and so far remains, soft on climate action and weak on stewardship of the environment.

But by this time, Canada had lived nine and a half years under a Stephen Harper–led Conservative government. The Harper Conservatives were disdainful of environmental protection, democratic principles, social justice, science, culture, and the truth. They passed "anti-terrorism" legislation that allowed government agencies to spy on whomever they liked and hold people in preventative detention (favoured targets were environmental and Indigenous activists). In 2011, Harper was the first and so far only Canadian prime minister to be found in contempt of Parliament. Four times he shut down Parliament to avoid debate. In the 2011 national election, the Conservatives violated election laws with fraudulent robocalls that suppressed the opposition vote. They then retroactively revised election laws and stripped Elections Canada – an independent, nonpartisan agency that reports to Parliament and is responsible for ensuring open and impartial elections – of its investigative powers.

With a majority of seats in the House, the Conservative government introduced massive omnibus bills that made sweeping legislative changes, which passed without debate. The Harper government utterly gutted environmental protections. They defunded our national broadcaster (the CBC) and took over its board with political appointees. They (he?) made ideological decisions to close government libraries, with such careless haste that documents with historical data on aquatic and polar ecosystems were dumped in landfills or burned before they could be digitized. Scientists were muzzled and history was revised. It seems almost unnecessary to add that Harper didn't consider climate change to be a real threat; he was pipeline pusher in chief. By 2015, a strong majority of Canadians wanted change.

An imperative to vote "strategically" befell those of us who value a healthy environment, social justice, democracy, science, the truth, and all that good stuff. In ridings across the country, the polling began as voters tried to discern which of the more progressive parties was best positioned to win particular ridings. There are strong distinctions between the Liberals, the NDP, and the Greens, but no matter which of the three one preferred, any of them would do to prevent the Conservatives from winning a majority of seats. Electing a Green would be as effective at preventing a Conservative majority as electing a Liberal or a New Democrat. At least, that is what I thought.

Across the country both the Liberals and the NDP promoted a storyline that extended strategic voting beyond the logic of preventing a Conservative majority: *Canadians! You must vote "strategically" for the party that can win the most seats in the election. To defeat the Conservatives, we (the NDP or the Liberals) must win a solid majority of seats. Don't "waste" your vote on a candidate whose party won't form government.* I was confused. When did minority governments become a bad thing? Isn't that how we got social security and universal healthcare? Why did it seem like everyone was accepting this logic?

Two weeks out from Election Day 2015, Dogwood, an environmental NGO, began to promote a small poll for Burnaby North–Seymour showing the NDP candidate in the lead. A week later, Leadnow, a democracy-focused

NGO, started promoting a more recent and larger poll showing the Liberal candidate in the lead. It was a more robust poll, but no poll can be predictive in such dynamic circumstances. With two opposing polls being heavily promoted with ads on social media right up to the day before election day, what was a strategic voter to do? At our final all-candidates meeting, I was mocked for my suggestion that perhaps the best "strategy" was to vote for the candidate you think will best represent you. In what sort of democracy is it silly to vote for your preferred candidate? Ours, apparently.

That same week, an angry, red-faced man accosted me on the sidewalk near the campaign office. He jabbed his finger at me and said, "I'll hold you personally responsible if Harper wins again." He raised his voice. "You are selfish! You are putting your own career ahead of what is good for the country." I stood and listened and did not tell him I was putting a career I love at risk for the good of the country. "If you don't withdraw your candidacy you will split the vote. You will be stealing votes from the NDP and the Conservatives will win."

Those who expressed a willingness to vote for me were similarly berated and bullied. Nathaniel Christopher wrote a comment on Facebook about his experience of volunteering with my campaign: "I was a flamboyantly gay teen in a small town in the '90s. I faced bullying and harassment. In 2015, I 'came out' as a Green supporter because I believed Lynne was the best candidate in our riding. For the first time in years, I was once again subjected to intense bullying. This time it came from NDP supporters, both online and in person." What a quagmire of divisiveness and cynicism.

When candidates are elected on the basis of negative campaigning, they are less accountable – they don't keep promises because they were not elected for their promises. Meanwhile, aberrant party discipline and corporate infiltration foster a tidy consolidation of power. We need to take Thomas King's advice and choose more carefully the stories we listen to.

As an advocate for women in science, I read studies conducted in business settings, which revealed that the best decisions are made by diverse groups of people working together with mutual respect. As an educator, I learned of similar work showing the value of team-based learning in the classroom. All of these studies translate well to politics. What they tell us is that no one person or small group of people has sufficient perspective, expertise, and disposition to effectively make wise decisions about complex issues – climate change, for example. I ran for the Green Party, but I do not claim that the Green Party is the be-all and end-all answer to everything. However, they are (so far) the only party in Canada that has made climate change their highest priority. We need more Green voices at the table. Who, I wonder, stands to gain when Green candidates are vilified and Green votes suppressed?

I was crushed by the campaign. The bullying and negative campaigning by the NDP was beyond anything I had ever experienced. It was exhausting. It didn't help that I was also exhausted from trying to do too much. Typically, after a full day of work at the university, I'd go straight to the campaign office for an evening of door-to-door canvassing. Like virtually everyone who has ever stood for election, I believed what I was doing was important and worth the sacrifices.

One particular day, home by nine thirty in the evening, I sat at my computer to review files for the next day's meetings at the university. It got late and I was still at my desk – I suppose I thought I was working on the campaign, as though writing hasty, angst-riddled posts online about climate change was somehow advancing the cause. I knew I should go to bed. I just couldn't muster the energy. I startled when a "ding" alerted me to an incoming message from a trusted friend: "You need to stop posting on Facebook at two a.m. It makes you look pathetic." I sighed, shaking my head at the strangeness of being watched at two in the morning. I glanced at the unmade bed in the corner of my one-room suite, piles of papers on the table, clothes strewn about, a pile of frozen pizza boxes, dirty dishes (mostly coffee mugs) piled in the sink. I felt pathetic. I was trying to run a political campaign without experienced staff, completely without experience myself, and in a riding where my party had no previous presence. And I was doing this without a partner. Jacob's dad and I had been good partners and that is what made it possible for me to build a career in academic science while raising a son. But now I was on my own, working a more than full-time job and running a federal election campaign on the heels of pipeline protests and lawsuits. I was exhausted before the campaign began.

On reflection, what happened with me was darker than simply getting worn down. Frustration and anger from the negative campaigning triggered a deeper awareness of the limits of our species. In 2015, I believed – perhaps needed to believe – that the public was hungry for real action on the climate crisis, that they would vote for action. The realization that I was wrong, that people were not ready to make climate a priority – or that they were manipulated away from this priority – triggered anguish. I've carried a general sadness about human-caused environmental degradation virtually my entire life. In this moment, I felt the deep truth that for many things I love, humanity will not act in time. The greater anguish was in knowing that things could have been different.

After the 2015 election, a parliamentary committee spent four months hearing from numerous expert witnesses and from citizens across the country and the answer was clear. A diversity of voices brought to Parliament through a proportional electoral system would serve our country well. Prime Minister Justin Trudeau was swept into power in part on his promise of electoral reform. As he said many times on the campaign trail, "This will be the last election under first past the post." He formed the committee, the parliamentarians did the work, and then he ignored their recommendations, declaring that electoral reform is "not in the best interests of the country." In our hijacked democracy, he has the power to single-handedly arbitrate what is "in the best interests of the country."

As I write this, the current small group of people in power have taken modest action on climate (instituting a carbon tax), while continuing to subsidize the fossil fuel industry and failing to build a robust transition plan. They have retained emissions targets set by the climate change-denying Harper government – targets that fall well below what would be needed to achieve our Paris commitments. Meanwhile, another small group – who may form the next government – complain that Canada only contributes about 2 per cent of global emissions, so why should we do anything at all when other countries are not acting. (Never mind that our per capita emissions are among the highest on the globe.) Without proportional representation, how do we break free from these swings of the pendulum that are not much change at all when it comes to climate action?

The extent to which corporate interests control our governments, regulatory agencies, and media outlets is unprecedented. In the introduction to his 2017 book, *Captured: The Corporate Infiltration of American Democracy*, Sheldon Whitehouse writes:

I've had a close-up look at government – as a prosecutor, as a regulator, as a government staffer, as a reformer, as a candidate, and as an elected official. Never in my life have I seen such influence in our elections from corporations and their managers and billionaire owners. Their presence in American elections has exploded, indeed become dominant, as the campaign finance world has become virtually lawless.

Never in my life have I seen such a complex web of front groups sowing deliberate deceit to create public confusion about issues that should be clear. The corporate propaganda machinery is of unprecedented size and sophistication.

Never in my life have I seen our third branch of government, our courts, the place in our governmental system that is supposed to be most immune from politics, under such political sway. The track record of the Supreme Court in particular shows patterns that are completely inconsistent with disinterested neutrality.

Kevin Taft provides a Canadian perspective in his 2017 book, *Oil's Deep State: How the Petroleum Industry Undermines Democracy and Stops Action on Global Warming – In Alberta, and in Ottawa*. From Taft's introduction:

The reason governments have failed to respond to climate change by reducing carbon emissions is that the fossil fuel industry has worked very hard, both directly and indirectly, to oppose effective government responses. This book examines the capture of democratic institutions such as political parties, government bureaucracies, regulators, and universities, so that those institutions increasingly serve the interests not of democracy, science, or the public, but the interests of the fossil fuel industry, especially the oil industry.

How do we deconstruct a concentration of power that is vulnerable to pressure from special interest groups, such as the petroleum lobby? I propose that we start by questioning the source of stories such as those that vilify Green candidates. We can support parliamentarians who fight to retain their independent voices, helping them be less susceptible to party discipline. And we can remember – remember what it means to have a vibrant democracy and a rich and abundant natural world. We adapt too easily to diminishment.

EXPEDITION

Early afternoon, we pull anchor and sail further into Kongsfjorden, closer to another glacier, Kronebreen, which we explore in the Zodiacs. The face of the glacier towers over us with chalk-white peaks inlaid with veins of reddish-brown impurities. One enormous blue face appears to have recently calved. The face is smooth, deep indigo, like the surface of a lake on a clear blue day, but vertical instead of horizontal. Even after seeing so many glaciers, they continue to disorient me. The wall of the valley of the mountain next to this one is red-brown, iron-rich sedimentary rock. Clinging to the wall in rows high above sea level are chunks of ice. Sarah tells us that Kronebreen has receded two kilometres in the ten years she has been coming here. The water is thick with bergy bits from the size of baseballs to buses.

I'm in the same Zodiac as Jessamyn, a physicist who hails from Los Alamos, New Mexico, but is currently settling into a new assistant professor position at the National University of Ireland in Galway. Jessamyn's expertise is nanomaterials that mimic the function and connectivity of the brain, with the potential to build organic neuromorphic devices, such as self-healing materials or computers that use the architecture of neurons and the brain. It happens that Jessamyn also does stand-up and has promised to give us a tutorial in comedy. This afternoon she has us looking for the clearest, most bubble-free ice we can find. We're hauling chunks of ice out of the water and stacking them on the floor of the Zodiac. Jessamyn wants to use the ice to build a particle detector in her cabin.

Once we're all back aboard, the *Antigua* returns up the fjord towards the research station at Ny-Ålesund. The sky is clear and brilliant, and the ocean is the most dramatic blue we have seen. When I arrive on deck, I'm disappointed to hear I missed seeing a minke whale off to port. Suddenly, just ahead are the explosive tall spouts of blue whales. The tall spouts hang in the air like ghosts. I revel in watching the three whales travelling beside and ahead of us – one much smaller than the other two, based on the size of its spout. One of the large whales blows near where I'm standing on the starboard side of the foredeck. I see the back of its head, the spout, and then I watch the arc of its back roll, and roll, and continue to roll on until at last, the characteristic tiny hooked dorsal fin appears, followed by a final flip of the tail flukes. According to the timestamp on my camera, it's a full twelve seconds from the spout to the flip of the flukes. Imagine it. Close your eyes and count out the seconds as you imagine the whale rolling by – one thousand and one, one thousand and two ... one thousand and twelve. The enormity is stunning. Blue whales are the largest animals that have ever lived on the planet.

For about a century, from the time we had the technology to kill them, right up until they were on the brink of extinction, humankind hunted blue whales for their baleen, their blubber, and their meat. In 1966, the International Whaling Commission protected blue whales from commercial hunting. There is debate about how well they are recovering. We know little about their habits and it's very difficult to estimate how many are alive today. Using numbers on the NOAA Fisheries website, one can estimate that the current population of blue whales is 2 to 5 per cent of what it was pre-whaling. I can barely believe we have just seen a family of three.

It is early evening by the time we are moored to the dock at Ny-Ålesund, where we'll stay for the night. After a short walk around the research station, a few of us had gathered in *Antigua*'s salon for a drink. I went to bed around midnight, but now it's two thirty in the morning and I'm back up in the salon with insomnia, joining a few stragglers still at the bar. I step out onto the deck and into the daylight. I miss the dark and I especially miss the stars. One of the great pleasures of wilderness trips for me has always been the night sky – the absence of light pollution and the opportunity to peer deep into space, to experience the sheer numbers of stars, to contemplate the planets on which life might be evolving, worlds with manifestations of intelligence different from our own. Alas, there is no darkness in the Arctic in June. But today, I travelled for a while with a blue whale and her family.

ACTIVIST

When I was a small child, our family spent most summer weekends exploring the Gulf Islands in a twelve-foot wooden outboard my father built. I loved that little boat. In the fall, Dad would go on weekend-long fishing trips to the wilder west coast of Vancouver Island. The men would return with coolers full of large salmon. One photo shows my brother and me (maybe five and six years old) posing next to three large salmon strung through the gills on a pole. One of the fish is as big as my brother. Harvests like this were common. We would preserve the salmon in jars and line them up in the basement alongside the jars of fruits and vegetables from the garden. My mother excelled at putting up all the produce we could harvest: canned plums, applesauce, dill pickles, canned tomatoes, beets, and beans. There were boxes of potatoes, onions, and winter squash. Fresh from the garden we ate corn, carrots, parsnips, radishes, strawberries, and raspberries. Zucchini was baked into everything.

When I was older, we "moved up" to a fifteen-foot fibreglass boat. It had a convertible roof and cover so in no time it could be a floating tent. Now the whole family would go out for weekend fishing trips off the west coast. I remember lots of rainy days fishing from within that tent, but I most clearly recall one long afternoon trolling out of sight of land on a sunny and windless day, bobbing up and down on slow-rolling waves, twenty feet from trough to peak. At the bottom, green water all around; at the top, nothing but horizon. I was a teenager and this was the last place on Earth I wanted to be. Still, I was impressed my father knew the way home. One of my favourite ports on these trips was a little fishing village called Bamfield. There is a marine research station at Bamfield and I used to dream of living there (one summer, as a university student, I did).

I've known the Salish Sea and the western Pacific Ocean for over fifty years. I remember the abundance, not only of salmon, but also of clams, oysters, and abalone; I remember the tide pools rich with different species of sea anemone, starfish, snails, crabs, and algae. I've witnessed the loss of abundance and diversity. The starfish populations in particular have been decimated. Long before I knew of the spiritual and practical importance of cedar trees to the Coast Salish people, cedar was my favourite tree. I love the elegant sweep of its boughs, its softness, and its stature. As a teenager I wrote letters to politicians, pleading for them to protect the Nitinat Triangle from logging. Now, I watch as groves of cedar trees die with every too-hot, too-dry summer. I watch as the last swaths of old growth forests are clear-cut.

I developed a strong sense of belonging to the land and then I spent twenty years moving from place to place, chasing the career that unexpectedly brought me to Svalbard. Where I finally landed is not too far from where I began. My research lab and teaching responsibilities are at Simon Fraser University (SFU), on the top of Burnaby Mountain – a suburban mountain, rising only six hundred metres above sea level, but rising in cliffs above the inlet and with a rim of forests between the university community and the rest of the world, including the city of Vancouver just a few miles away. When I first arrived at SFU almost twenty years ago, the walk to my lab was along a path lined with salmon berries, blackberries (invasive, but delicious), huckleberries, salal, and Oregon grape. Two buildings now sit where the path once was, but the forest rimming the mountain remains a tranquil place filled with trails for an afternoon walk. What I didn't anticipate was that this land would come under a much greater threat than the slow creep of new buildings.

For two years after the coal train blockade, I kept my climate activism focused on coal exports. Climate scientists agree that to have a reasonable chance of avoiding a level of global warming that would trigger catastrophic climate change, coal and the so-called nonconventional fossil fuels, including fracked gas and tar sands, need to stay in the ground. There were few of us in British Columbia protesting coal and it felt like a good use of the limited time and energy I had available. But then diluted bitumen came knocking.

It started simply enough: I was invited to join a group (landowners, business people, academics, and environmental advocates) who were building a case to bring a legal challenge against Canada's National Energy Board (the NEB). We met with the lawyers in a large meeting room at the downtown Vancouver offices of a local NGO. The lawyer went around the table, interviewing us one by one about why we wanted to be part of this. He was probing for who might be the voices to lead the case. When it came to my turn, I calmly presented a sincere and solidly reasoned argument for why I would *not* be a good choice. The lawyer grinned.

On 6 May 2014, Quarmby, et al. filed a constitutional challenge to amendments of the National Energy Board Act made by the Conservative government of Stephen Harper. The changes removed consideration of upstream and downstream effects from the review of Kinder Morgan's proposal for a pipeline to carry 890,000 barrels per day of diluted bitumen from the Alberta tar sands to be loaded onto tankers in Burnaby, for export. In other words: climate change considerations were off the table.

Our position was that ignoring the impacts on climate change is inconsistent with the mandate to evaluate whether such a long-life project is in the broad public interest. We called for a public hearing, charging that the NEB amendments violated the public right to freedom of expression guaranteed by the Charter of Rights and Freedoms. I was quoted in a press release as saying, "The NEB seems to be determined that if it buries its head in the sand deep enough it can refuse to see what is absolutely clear to everyone around it. This motion invites the Board to come into the public realm, to confront the evidence that climate change is real and can't be ignored and to publicly state, if it dares, that it will continue to ignore reality. We hope that, given the opportunity, it will come to its senses and agree to conduct a full and proper inquiry into the wisdom of the Kinder Morgan application." We managed to keep the ball in the air until 10 September 2015, when the Supreme Court of Canada declined to hear our legal challenge.

While our challenge was making its way through the courts, the Kinder Morgan pipeline project came to dominate my life. Many precious days of my one life have been burned up fighting this project, fighting my own government. Why is a democratic government not pulling with us for the common good?

EXPEDITION

We spend the night moored at the Ny-Ålesund dock. In the salon after breakfast, Sarah gives a brief outline of plans for the day, as she has done every day. "Today you can wander Ny-Ålesund without an armed guide, but don't leave the station limits – there are signs." She grins. "All of the doors are unlocked so you can run into any building if you see a bear." Sarah has also arranged for us to participate in the launch of an international weather balloon at one o'clock. Until then, our time is our own.

We're little more than halfway through our expedition and I'm dismayed we have come out of the wilderness to be among people and buildings. Ny-Ålesund is an international scientific research station on the southern shore of Kongsfjorden. The morning is fresh and clear, and from shore I look east across green salt flats and the deep blue fjord to Kronebreen. From this distance its towering face is reduced to a well-defined shoreline, but its massive back stretches high and wide up the valley, glistening white. I imagine it emerging from a vast interior ice sheet like those I saw on the flight in. Mountains beyond the glacier are rocky and rise steeply into jagged, snowy peaks. Near the pier lies an abandoned coal train with a few wooden carts in tow on a short stretch of remaining track. My eye is repeatedly drawn beyond the train, back to the green salt flats; there is something evolutionary about how much I've missed the colour green.

I stroll the gravel path about one hundred metres to the centre of town – a cluster of colourfully painted wooden buildings connected by boardwalks and gravel paths. In the summer season, there are about two hundred people in residence. There are houses, a post office (the most northerly in the world), one store (a gift shop with junk food), a museum testifying to the history of mining and exploration, and a newer building dedicated to polar research. In the centre of the village is a larger-than-life bronze bust of Roald Amundsen, occupation: explorer. The Norwegian led the first expedition to the South Pole, from 1910 to 1912, and he was on board the airship *Norge* when she flew over the North Pole in 1926, making him the first man to visit both poles.

The Arctic tern is a tough little gull that migrates every year from the South Pole to the North Pole and back, chasing polar summer. The white body and black-capped head is punctuated with a bright red beak. It is a red that warns in the way that the red hourglass on the back of a black widow spider says, "Do not mess with me." It is a beak that says, "I am dripping with blood from the last mammalian skull I cracked." I catch up with some of the others, and as we walk through town we pull up our hoods and wave our hands over our heads to fend off these aggressive little balls of muscle and beak. They persistently dive bomb us, and I'm struck on the head several times, grateful to have my hood up. A scientist cycles by with a four-foot-long stick strapped to her handlebars. On the top of the stick is a stuffed glove.

I spot a tern sitting close to the path, camouflaged in the lichens, moss, and stones of the tundra, incubating an egg. Why has the tern colony moved into town? The penny drops when I wander away from the group to the edge of town and see the sign warning of polar bears beyond. With climate change impacting the bears' ability to hunt for seals on the ice, they must be turning to birds' eggs for sustenance. Already, the Arctic terns have learned that their eggs are safer in proximity to people.

Ny-Ålesund reminds me of the Bamfield of my youth. I fantasize about spending a year working at this remote research station, drawn by the views, the quiet, and the proximity to nature – annoying birds and all.

ON REASONS TO OPPOSE A PIPELINE

I can be as tenacious as an Arctic tern in my defence of nature. Sometimes the passion of my activism is misunderstood as fanaticism. It is not. There is a great deal of misinformation and propaganda about fossil fuel projects, including the Trans Mountain (Kinder Morgan) Pipeline and tanker expansion project. Because I don't want to be mistaken for a fanatic, I've made a list of some of the reasons I oppose this pipeline. In a compassionate, rational world, any *one* of these reasons would be enough to stop this project. The list isn't exhaustive, but even so it is varied and sordid, raising serious questions about the morality of a democratic government – the Government of Canada – that not only approved this project, but is subsidizing it with taxpayer dollars (and in fact, in 2018, purchased the pipeline).

Here are the main reasons I am adamantly opposed to the Trans Mountain Pipeline expansion – many of them apply to fossil fuel infrastructure projects around the globe:

1 A large fraction of the oil sands (or tar sands) are developed using an open-pit mining process that requires complete removal of the "over burden," otherwise known as boreal forest. The boreal forest is Earth's most efficient land-based "carbon capture" system – fully functioning, cost-effective negative emissions – and Canada is actively destroying it.

2 Processing the mined bitumen is energy intensive and toxic. The tar, or bitumen, is combined with "diluent" – a mixture of volatile, flammable neurotoxins and carcinogens, including benzene – to make "dilbit" (diluted bitumen), a substance that can flow in a pipeline. Newer oil sands development involves bitumen extraction by an *in situ* process wherein the tar is "steamed" out of the sand and collected in pipes underground. Both processes involve massive quantities of toxins and both are energy-intensive projects with substantial carbon dioxide emissions. Not only do the fossil fuel companies in the tar sands get a pass on the "externality" of polluting the atmosphere, they receive substantial subsidies.

3 Processing bitumen requires not only energy, but also vast quantities of water. Much of it comes from the Athabasca River, fed by a rapidly retreating glacier, which is being diverted and converted into toxic sludge.

4 There is meant to be "reclamation" of the land post-extraction. Yet, after decades of expansion and retiring of old sites, we have acre upon acre of stinking, toxic tailings ponds, where loud cannons fire frequently to keep waterfowl from landing and dying. A small percentage of the land has been remediated to something better than a tailings pond, leaving little more than a species-poor grassland with nothing resembling the peaty soil and biodiversity of a boreal forest, which will take hundreds of years to return, if ever.

5 Indigenous people living in northern Alberta and Saskatchewan, some of them literally downstream from the tar sands on the Athabasca River, have had their air, water, and land polluted and their way of life threatened. In a 2012 article in the *International Journal of Human Rights*, Jennifer Huseman and Damien Short carefully outline the evidence for impacts of oil sands development on the Indigenous peoples of northern Alberta. Their conclusion: "Many people in Indigenous communities feel that they are in the final stages of a battle

for survival that began in North America in the seventeenth century, and have called their past and present situation, brought on by settlers and colonial governments, genocide. Their use of the term is not emotive or imprecise, but ... highlights the enormity of what the tar sands are doing to the Indians of Treaty 8 and beyond." I am deeply troubled that these atrocities are by government design and supported by tax dollars.

6 Pipelines leak. They rupture, they break, accidents happen. And when dilbit is in the pipeline, the consequences are significant, as the people of Kalamazoo, Michigan, will tell you after experiencing just such a spill in 2010. They can never return to homes infused with toxic fumes from the volatile diluent. In 2007, there was a pipeline accident in Burnaby. That one was "just" oil, but try telling the people who experienced it that it was not so bad. Accidents happen not infrequently – there have been thirteen spills along the Trans Mountain Pipeline since Kinder Morgan took it over in 2005, as documented on the company's own "spill history" webpage. Thanks to "streamlined" environmental regulations by our previous Conservative government under Stephen Harper (retained by the current Liberal government), accidents will be more frequent and more consequential. This might explain how Kinder Morgan can get away with laying anti-spawning mats in the streams it proposed to cross. *See, there are no salmon in this stream. This is a good place for our pipeline.* When people found the mats, the company was barely given a slap on the wrist (a $920 fine).

7 Almost one third of the proposed pipeline route crosses the territory of the Secwepemc Nation. Driven by the economic pressures of deprivation, some band councils signed benefit agreements with Kinder Morgan, yet, as I heard at a recent gathering held on the bank of the Thompson River where the pipeline crosses, there is vehement disagreement about this project among the Secwepemc. Similarly strong opposition

is found along the route, climaxing with the Tsleil-Waututh Nation, in whose territory the tankers will fill at the terminus of the pipeline. The NEB review process and subsequent hearings for the pipeline egregiously neglected the need for prior and informed consent from First Nations.

8 On the southwest side of Burnaby Mountain is a "tank farm" where product is stored as it continues to flow, awaiting the arrival of a tanker to fill. This is not a "farm" as in a place where things are nurtured and grown. It is the opposite. Like the old pipeline, this tank farm is too small to accommodate the tripling of product that is proposed to flow to the coast. The project proposes installing new, larger tanks *between* the existing ones, obliterating the buffer zone around each tank, which the original design featured in order to prevent a fire in one tank from spreading catastrophically. When built, the tank farm was in the middle of nowhere, but Burnaby has grown up around it and now the tank farm is near a subdivision, an elementary school, and the only road to and from the university on top of the mountain (the university where I work). Comments from the Burnaby Fire Department have been scathing, outlining the risks associated with the proposed densification of tanks full of highly flammable materials and volatile neurotoxins near a forest that is tinder-dry in the summer, all in an earthquake zone. What could possibly go wrong? That the Canadian federal government would approve a project that makes a sacrifice zone of an elementary school, a suburban neighbourhood, and a university doesn't sound like democracy to me.

9 At the tanker port in Burnaby, an Aframax-class tanker will be filling every day. Well, not quite filling, because a full tanker would scrape bottom as it navigated the narrow passage under the Iron Workers Memorial Bridge leaving the inlet. The Tsleil-Waututh people have been working hard to restore the pristine waters that fed their nation for thousands of years. They vociferously do not give their consent to this project.

10 The tankers will pass through the Salish Sea, home of a population of resident orca whales, sensitive to the sounds of shipping and already starving from diminished salmon stocks. And of course, there is the issue of tanker spills. Spills do and will happen. Our federal government assures us we have a "world-class spill response." Sadly, that doesn't mean much. A study from the National Academy of Sciences (in the US) shows that spilled bitumen is likely to sink, while the volatile diluent chemicals will float in the air as a highly flammable and toxic cloud. Indeed, this is what was observed with the Kalamazoo spill. Recovery is a fantasy, a delusion. The myth of clean-up is propaganda generated by those who don't give a damn.

11 The dilbit is delivered to ports in the US where there are special facilities that can handle the gooey tar so it can be refined and shipped to Asia or piped to users in the US. Wherever it ends up, the tar from Alberta will be burned, and converted into usable energy (heat, electricity), and lots of carbon dioxide. Climate science is clear on this: as a society, we need to stop increasing our emissions by 2020 and cut them by almost 50 per cent every decade thereafter. We need to transition off coal as soon as possible, and nonconventional fossil fuels that require almost as much energy to recover as they yield, such as the bitumen of the Athabasca tar sands – these need to stay in the ground.

Why has the Government of Canada approved a pipeline with a thirty- to fifty-year lifespan, to allow *expanded* operations in the tar sands? Why are they so determined to push it through?

I understand that in a democracy, different people will have different priorities and that compromise is often appropriate. But where is the leadership that would shift subsides from a dying industry into job training in new sectors such as renewable energy, retrofitting of buildings for energy efficiency, and the transition to new approaches to agriculture that will sequester more carbon? I am tired of being told I am naïve and that these things cannot be done. I've seen the data from Canada and other countries – I know it absolutely can and needs to be done.

EXPEDITION

When we gather near the weather station for the launch of the weather balloon, the scientists invite two of our group to participate. Pablo and Rachael climb the stairs to the launch pad – it looks a bit like a loading dock, with a large pull-down door to keep the weather out between launches, and an open deck with free access to the sky for the launch itself. We watch the balloon inflate to its approximately six-foot diameter. When it is fully inflated, Pablo holds the bottom of the balloon while a scientist attaches the instruments. Rachael is holding a horizontal pole, at each end of which dangles a cord attached to various measuring instruments.

It makes me happy to hear the scientist describe to this group of artists that "It takes a two-year overlap of duplicate technology whenever we upgrade our instruments. We must know the precise relationship between data being gathered now and data gathered in the past." Suddenly there is a rush to get things going – the balloon must be launched within a fifteen-minute window to coordinate with balloon launches around the world. We watch it carry the instruments high up into the atmosphere, sending back data as it rises.

By mid-afternoon, the *Antigua* casts off from Ny-Ålesund with favourable winds and a long run ahead of us. We'll be sailing south in the open water on the outside of Forlandsundet, an island off the west coast of Spitsbergen. As we leave the fjord, we're gathered on deck and everyone is assigned a task. Ludo is teaching a small group of us how to pull or to play out rope, how to coil and loop and knot, as appropriate: "… then bring this end up and through. Like this." He's patient and good-humoured as we clumsily try to mimic his polished moves. "Now, wrap the free end, then back down and through. See?" This is the first time we're raising the sails and I begin to appreciate the sophisticated system of ropes and pulleys, booms and sails of this beautiful tall ship. "Now pull tight and hang it on this hook." First and second mates, Paulien and Alwin, are up in the rigging, coaxing sails this way and that. In small teams, we heave on cue and up goes a sail, catching the wind and unfurling as we haul, coil, and stow the rope. Finally, I understand why Captain Joe has been so fussy about conditions – a good wind and a distant landing – before raising the sails. It's a major undertaking. But oh, what a feeling to be under wind power! It seems everyone is in a good mood.

Dill pickle pizza for dinner and now I'm relaxing on my cot. I've excused myself from the crowded salon where we had gathered for another round of artist talks. I love being under sail, but this is our first time in relatively open water and I'm seasick. Knowing from experience how unpleasant the nausea can get, I didn't want to stay in the cramped, closed space of the salon. After some time on deck in the fresh air, gazing at the horizon, I retreated to my cot and lay down with my eyes closed. I'm sad to be missing the talks, but after an hour or so of being horizontal without visual input, I'm feeling better. The break from constant stimulation is also a relief.

Seasickness is caused when our senses send our brain mixed messages – our vestibular system is telling us one thing while our visual system provides conflicting information. Living as we did in evolutionary time – walking the land or climbing trees – information from the labyrinth of our inner ear, with its keen sensitivity to motion and position, works together with visual information from our eyes to feed our brains with a constant awareness of our changing position during movement. But when that movement is something beyond our evolutionary experience – travel on a ship, a car, or a plane – our inner ear can't keep up with the rate of change of position as we bounce up and down or speed along a highway. Information from our eyes conflicts with signals from our inner ears and we experience confusion about the position and motion of our body in space.

In a strange way, seasickness is a gift – a relatively rare opportunity for awareness of the fallibility of our senses, direct experiential knowledge that they can fail to convey accurate information about our world. When we have this experience, we say we're car sick, motion sick, or seasick. Seasickness: nausea induced by awareness of delusion.

Occasionally, when I think about business-as-usual political decisions or unjust legal decisions that favour corporations at the expense of future generations, or marginalized populations or the environment, I feel a bit nauseated. In the past I've put it down to anxiety, eco-anxiety, state-of-the-world anxiety. Now I wonder, might it be a form of "awareness-of-delusion sickness"? Like all human brains, mine unconsciously filters inputs so I can function. One of those filters is: *do I trust the source?* Over evolutionary time, leaders of our communities were trusted to guide us, to find ways forward that would best serve the whole group. Today, the information we're receiving from our traditionally trustworthy sources, such as elected leaders and mainstream media, is at odds with information we're receiving from other trusted sources, such as scientists, independent investigative journalists, and others. I feel nausea because I am aware our society is being led by people who are not trustworthy.

ACTIVIST

On the morning of 3 September 2014, a little over a year before the federal election, I was in my office when in short succession I received several messages from activist friends and from my colleague and friend Stephen Collis. Word came in by email, text, and direct message: "Kinder Morgan is on the mountain. They have cut down trees in the woods below the rose garden." "They're just off Gnome's Home trail." "They are surveying for the pipeline. Can you come?" I postponed my afternoon meetings and walked across campus and down a wooded path to the rose garden and the sloping, open grassy area of Burnaby Mountain Park. The park has a spectacular view over Vancouver, Burrard Inlet, and the North Shore mountains, but on this particular day, clouds obscured the view. Nevertheless, before me was a stunning scene as I came through the rose garden: a small crowd of protesters gathering near the cluster of totem poles known as Playground of the Gods. These totems are unusual for our area – Toko Nuburi, an Ainu, indigenous to northern Japan, carved them. They represent gods descending to create the world.

I recognized a few friends among the protesters and a journalist from the local paper, *Burnaby Now*. I learned that a Kinder Morgan survey crew had been on the mountain in the very early hours of the morning and cut down thirteen trees in the Burnaby conservation forest, just below where we were gathered. Park officials were asking people not to trek down the muddy trail to the site for fear that too many people on the trail in the mud would damage the forest. Cutting down the trees was in violation of Burnaby bylaws.

Over the following weeks, a small group of us started taking turns sitting vigil in the forest, near the stumps.

> A raven announces territory
> As deep distancing echo
> Gnome's are not seen
> But they are evening
> Shadow on mountain trail
> Black bears amble to
> Forage beneath blue
> Heavens above clearing
> Where thirteen trees lie
> On forest floor and thirteen
> Shadows still hold up the sky
> Holding off the helicopter world
> Dropping – bituminous – in their midst
> – Stephen Collis, from "Thirteen Trees,"
> in *Once in Blockadia*

One day in the woods, sitting on a log, a young First Nation man generously shared his story. Having lived in the US from 1985 to 2000, I had missed a great deal of Canadian news – Canada was awaking to a history that wasn't taught when I was a child nor acknowledged when I was a young adult. Slowly, on my return to Canada, I was piecing together an understanding of the disturbing colonial history of this place. Listening to Adam talking about his experience as part of the "Sixties Scoop" (which continued well into the 1980s), in which Indigenous children were pulled from their homes and raised by white families, my understanding deepened.

Having grown up rural and definitely not wealthy, I resisted the label "privileged." Being the fourth generation of my family grounded in this place, I also resisted the label "settler." But I was learning of residential schools, of genocide, and of the trauma experienced by Indigenous people who lived just down the road when I was growing up; I was hearing the strong, clear voices of people who were invisible to me when I was young; I was learning what it really meant to belong to the land. I came to recognize my privilege and responsibilities. I now own the label "settler," and as I find my way towards reconciliation, I see that true reconciliation will be as difficult to face as climate change. One thing I can do that serves both reconciliation and climate change is defend the land, air, and water from a corporate system that views nature as an economic externality.

As we sat vigil in the woods, Stephen and I talked about what we were going to do when Kinder Morgan returned. We talked about how to bring more people to the mountain. Stephen was writing and doing interviews and we were all working to get the word out on social media. The protest was growing. When we learned Trans Mountain was planning a second drilling site on the mountain (for a geological survey in anticipation of tunnelling through the mountain), we relocated the focus of the protest to this site, on the side of a small road that led up to the rose garden.

One dark, rainy Friday night after work, I stopped to support those on site – at that time there were just two young men camping in the back of a pickup truck. "How are you guys doing?" "Great! Well … a bit wet and cold." Only after I promised to stay and occupy the space until they returned did the two young men drive off for a hot meal. I sat in my car alone, listening to the rain, looking out into the dark woods and thinking, "This is silly. Kinder Morgan isn't going to show up tonight." A car drove slowly by and then again, a few minutes later, on its way back down the mountain. I shivered and remained on the site waiting for the return of my confederates.

EXPEDITION

We sailed through the night, and this morning my seasickness has subsided. After breakfast we listen to more talks. Sarah is confident and strong when in the role of expedition leader, but she is quiet and understated when talking about her art. She shows us stills from a performance piece, a video played on exhibit in Europe, images with words: "*I will be at Longyearbyen airport, waiting for every incoming flight. (I'll be wearing a turquoise blue dress.) … It's not warm here, that's true, but I've bought you a very good sleeping bag. Come … I've learned how to shoot now. I will protect you against polar bears. Come whenever you want. I am here. I am waiting.*" And every day for the duration of the show, Sarah put on her blue dress and met every incoming flight at the Longyearbyen airport.

With quiet confidence, Rachael takes command of the room. A composer, a sound artist, and a performer, Rachael is highly accomplished, and I'm enthralled as she presents snippets from various projects, sampling her compositions. Rachael's work focuses on grief around human death and on space exploration. She is onto something that resonates with me; I hold the feeling but not her words. I'll later look up her webpage and find that she seeks to elicit in her audience something akin to the cognitive shift "reported by astronauts and cosmonauts during orbit due to their privileged ability to see the earth from a distance." She notes that this "type of enlightenment is often mimicked through the process of dying, and for the surrounding mourners in human death." Seeing Earth from a distance. Facing death, or the death of a loved one. These are perspectives that help us feel the transience of our individual lives.

We're called on deck to help bring the sails down. There is some hesitation – we have already been trained how to tie knots and stow ropes, but we're a long way from mastery and insecure about our skills. Soon there is laughter as Ludo makes the rounds, inspecting the mess we've made of things. "No, no," he laughs. "*Around* and *then* back down through the loop. Like this." He guides our reparations. "That's it! Deidre's got it!" There is lightness in the mood and I suddenly realize it's much warmer and the water is ice-free; we have sailed south into a different climatic zone. We're in Bellsund, and, under a brilliant ultramarine sky, we prepare for an afternoon landing at Camp Bell. We talk of sunglasses and sunscreen. Because the light is so intense, I add a neutral density filter to my camera lens.

There are big patches of soggy snow ripe for snow algae, but alas, they are all white. I walk around for a bit and find decaying whale vertebrae and rib bones. I wonder, how old? Which of the large species? What death? Small ponds, lush green moss – everything is soaked in snowmelt. The colours are intense: bleached-white bone, chlorophyll-green moss, ultramarine sky, and indigo sea decorated with whitecaps. I take lots of photos and then find a grassy nook sheltered from the wind by a large rock, and warmed by the sun hitting the lee side of the same rock. I take off my parka and spread it out on the ground. I unload my backpack onto the parka – notebook and pen, water bottle, camera, wool headband, and a tube of pomegranate lip balm (Arctic air is very dry). Once empty, my padded backpack makes an excellent backrest against the rock. I settle into this nest, sitting on my parka in the warm sun with the notebook on my lap and pen in hand. I feel good. It's a glorious day.

As soon as I'm settled, I begin to wonder how hard I looked for watermelon snow. I'm confident if there'd been a full bloom, I would've seen it. But was I looking closely enough to notice the subtle early stages? Was I sure I hadn't missed something? I start to get anxious, and then relax – it's okay. I'm soaking up the experience of being here. I remind myself that my real science is back home, understanding the alpine snow algae microbiome of my local mountains. Finding Arctic snow algae would have been exciting and I would have loved to photograph the living cells through the microscope. I might have made meaningful observations about their *in situ* morphology, but I am thinking more of their beauty than the science. I know that the artists on this trip would have flipped to see the living microscopic jewels. Oh, well. With or without the algae,

I'm confident that I'll make something of the precious experience of being here. My discomfort is that I don't know yet what it will be.

I have had enough of the bright sun. I long for the quieting fog and subtleties of grey light and ethereal blue ice of northern Svalbard. We still have five more days of travel on the *Antigua*, yet here in the warm sun, there is a sense we have turned homeward. I'm not ready. Today's jarring brightness is like the Sun poking me with a stick – yes, I'm here shining day and night. I'm intense and I'm not going away. The persistence of the light suddenly feels oppressive, like a problem that won't go away, like the truth about global warming.

Back on the *Antigua*, I'm keen to look at my photos from today – the saturated blues of sea and sky, the greens of moss and grass, the bleached-white whale bones. When I open the files, every shot is dark in the corners and edges forming a heavy vignette. How did I not notice this when I was shooting? What has happened? I'm perplexed and ask others for an explanation. Tentatively, Eric mentions he noticed me stacking filters and was not sure whether he should say anything. It's a rookie mistake. Oh, how I wish he had spoken up. Oh, how I regret not soliciting more advice earlier on the trip. Piled on to my desire to return to the northern tip of Spitsbergen is now a craving to have a second chance to photograph the ice.

ACTIVIST

On 25 October 2014, almost two months after Kinder Morgan cut down the thirteen trees in the conservation forest on Burnaby Mountain, I published an op-ed in the *Vancouver Observer*. The piece was sensationalized, with a photo of my arrest during the train blockade, and a headline that proclaimed my willingness to get arrested to stop the pipeline. I wrote:

> In the past 24 hours tensions have been rising as we anticipate the return of Kinder Morgan with an injunction and orders for us to be arrested … The only world in which it is okay to continue building new infrastructure for fossil fuels with no consideration for climate change is a world where we don't care about the future, or about other places on the globe, or about disappearing species, or about ocean acidification. I live in a world where we care about these things. And in my world we have a moral obligation to do everything in our power to stop construction of new fossil fuel infrastructure that is approved without consideration of the cumulative effects on climate change.

Stephen and I went looking for attention, and we got it. It was five o'clock on a Thursday, five days after my op-ed was published, when I heard a disturbance in the outer departmental offices. I emerged from my office to find the staff gathered around my assistant, who handed me a four-inch stack of paper. "A man who didn't say who he was just handed this to me and asked me to give it to you." I was stunned to see my name and the words "Supreme Court of BC" on the front page. Stephen's name was there, too, along with three others, including Adam, a passionate young woman named Mia, and Alan, an older man who hadn't actually been protesting on the mountain, but who was named as the representative of a local residents' association that had been battling the pipeline since the 2007 leak, long before I was involved.

The delivery was followed by an email with more volumes of attachments. It took a bit of digging to discover that the Kinder Morgan subsidiary Trans Mountain was suing us for "tortious interference," although the specific cases varied. We were due in court at two thirty the following afternoon. We started scrambling to find lawyers, but the first thing I did was call a journalist. Outrage trumped fear.

We spent that Friday afternoon and four days the following week in court, defending against the suit for a purported $5.6 million in lost revenue caused by us sitting in the park and inviting others to join us. Trans Mountain had been spying on us for weeks and it was creepy to see in evidence long-lens photographs of the four of us in the park, occupying the space the company wanted to occupy. Much of the evidence against us was absurd.

Some of Stephen's lyrical writing was read out in court – as evidence for what, wasn't clear, although the Trans Mountain lawyer implied that perhaps encoded in Stephen's words were instructions for how to build a barricade. Also presented in evidence was a photo of a jack-o'-lantern carved with the words "No Pipelines." Sitting alongside protest signs at the growing encampment on the mountain, the pumpkin was presented as evidence of intimidation of the survey crew by the protestors. Really? The surveyors were afraid of our pumpkin? The judge accepted the evidence with gravity while I was having a hard time keeping a straight face – the urge to laugh mixed potently with intense frustration.

The survey crew also claimed that some of the protestors made scary faces that they found intimidating. This triggered #KMFace, used by supporters to tweet "scary face" selfies. People were having lots of fun with it on social media, but I resisted the cajoling because I was too self-conscious to have an ugly photo of me circulating on the Internet. Eventually, I gave in to the desire to be a good sport. A friend said, "C'mon. Show us the face that made Kinder Morgan so afraid of Lynne Quarmby that they sued to shut you up." I snarled, he snapped, and the photo entered the Twittersphere. When the *Vancouver Sun* ran a profile of the protestors, the paper accompanied the paragraph about me with that ugly photo, with no reference to #KMFace, just an ugly face that revealed the criminal nature of this miscreant. The judge nodded gravely as a powerful pipeline company presented its evidence of intimidation by protestors: one scary jack-o'-lantern, poetry with hidden meaning, and some ugly faces. The court case felt surreal, like I was living in a dystopian fiction.

During a ten-day wait for the judge's decision, the protest continued to grow and several of us were doing a lot of media interviews. The protest encampment sprouted additions to its makeshift shelters, and barricades built of debris salvaged from the forest grew higher and more complex. The site was occupied twenty-four hours a day, and supportive community members came by with hot meals and bags of fresh fruit. I brought hot coffee in the mornings on my way to work.

Banners, signs, pumpkins, and chalk on the road all made clear that this community opposed the pipeline. Daytime crowds were swelling into the hundreds, and one evening rally drew around a thousand people. Eventually, the anticipated result was confirmed: the judge ruled in favour of Trans Mountain and issued an injunction to keep protestors out of the park. This was a SLAPP (a strategic lawsuit against public participation), and in this jurisdiction (as in many others) the corporations (almost) always win.

I took a call from a Canadian Press reporter immediately after the decision was announced. The reporter asked, "Would you do this again, now you know the consequences?" What? Did she think I was some child who hadn't understood the consequences of misbehaviour? I was incensed by what I took to be her implicit agreement with the decision. Did she think I would give up my voice, stop speaking up for what is right, just because our legal system is rigged to favour corporations? Writing about it now, I wonder if perhaps she had meant to ask whether the decision was going to have the intended effect of silencing me. Either way, I think she got her answer from my angry rant. I was not about to be silenced.

We waited for the RCMP to act. It was cold, wet winter weather, and it was obvious their strategy was to wait for the crowds to dwindle before they came in to make arrests and set up their line of defense on behalf of the corporation. A few days later, in the early hours of the morning, the RCMP arrived and began arresting the determined group camping on the site. Some had chained themselves to concrete blocks at the roadside site; one was doing a tree-sit down the hill at the forest site. I got a call that it was going down and arrived as soon as I could.

The scene was chaotic and frightening. People running through the woods, yelling, police struggling to take control of the space, protesters struggling to hold the same space. In one video interview I'm crying – tears of frustration at the injustice. Corporations can manipulate public opinion and sometimes even buy scientists, but money can't change science – hard realities like how much carbon dioxide is in the atmosphere. I'm often filled with self-doubt, but this is one thing I know with confidence: time will show that those protesting this pipeline are on the right side of history. With the mountain cleared of protesters, that night Trans Mountain arrived with trailers of heavy equipment for drilling into the mountain, protected at both sites by chain-linked fence and a police line.

I faced a difficult decision: Would I cross the injunction line and risk arrest? Without a phone call from veteran environmentalist and organizer Karen Mahon, I might not have considered the question. Karen gently helped me appreciate the public profile I had built during the protests. I had been so focused on the cause that I failed to appreciate the obvious fact that by doing so many interviews, people weren't just learning about the happenings on Burnaby Mountain, they were getting to know me. That I'm a middle-class, middle-aged professional woman helped refute those who argued that the protestors were "fringe."

Karen said something about organizing a press conference for the next morning, but before committing, I needed time to think and to consult. There was still a $5.6 million lawsuit hanging over my head and I was concerned my prior arrest for blockading the coal train might motivate the courts to make an example of me. Violation of an injunction can be a civil charge, but if done "flagrantly," criminal charges may be sought. If I violated the injunction, it most certainly would be flagrant, and criminal charges could mean jail time or a large fine, and a criminal record that could cause difficulty crossing into the US, where my son Jacob lives. Friends advised that I really did not need to do this. I had done enough already and others could now step up. But then I called Jacob. After all, it was he who stood to lose his financial safety net if I were to lose my condo and my retirement savings. "Do it, Mom," he said. "There is nothing you could do for my future that is more important than this."

EXPEDITION

After an hour's travel from Camp Bell, we have arrived at Fridtjofhamna. At dinner Sarah announces, "Tonight we'll celebrate the summer solstice with a party on the beach." There is general approval and good spirits, but the real cheering comes when she adds, "Tomorrow morning there will be a late brunch. You can all sleep in and spend the morning relaxing." I've been feeling dazed by the constant flux of new experiences, and like everyone else I'm grateful for a little slack in the schedule.

Winter solstice is one of my favourite days of the year. I love a winter bonfire, potluck dinner with friends, music and poetry, kids and laughter, and the knowledge that longer, warmer days are ahead. The true dawning of a new year, winter solstice stirs feelings of renewal and anticipation. In contrast, summer solstice has always felt bittersweet to me – a luxuriously long day that marks the beginning of the slide back to short, stubby little days. I've been in the Arctic just two weeks and my views of the solstices have completely shifted. I'm drained by the constant daylight; I long for a dark sky, a real night. Summer solstice is suddenly something to celebrate.

We're shuttled by Zodiac to shore. I'm amazed at the amount of drift-wood we salvage in this treeless land. Soon, a bonfire is blazing. Justin has arranged a "blue nose" ceremony. According to him, everyone who crosses the eightieth parallel earns a blue nose. We didn't quite make it that far north, but close – very close! He has concocted a beautiful Arctic-blue cream that he ceremoniously dabs on the tip of each nose.

In the golden light of the midnight sun, Louise glows like a Vermeer portrait – standing on a small hill of golden pebbles a short distance from the partiers, she is framed by distant mountains and sky; she stands tall and straight, scanning the horizon, rifle hung over her shoulder. In the foreground, Nemo is curled into a tight ball, every hair in golden relief. Around the fire there are stories and laughter, and eventually dancing, fire leaping, and swimming.

I am delighted that I manage to sleep late. I take my time getting up and dressed, and almost miss even the extended breakfast time. Since Risa pointed them out to me, I've been enjoying the perfectly prepared medium-soft boiled eggs. This morning I am too late for an egg, but in addition to the usual spread, there are waffles! It is a treat to move slowly. By the time I return to my room to dress properly for the day, the *Antigua* is underway.

It is a short, thirty-minute trip further down the fjord to Fridtjofbreen, where we set anchor for the afternoon. Back up in the salon, Sarah gives us three options for our landing. One group will be landing on the east side of the glacier, where Tims will lead them up and onto the ice for a walk across the top of the glacier. Back home in BC, I've had the experience of walking on a glacier – it was fascinating, but filled with more tension than I am in the mood for this afternoon. A second group will have a stationary landing on a small beach on the west side of the glacier.

I'm filled with a desire to move over the landscape – to stride and breathe – so I choose the third option of a hike up the gentle ridge, a lateral moraine left by the retreating glacier on the west side of the bay. The plan is to hike to a peak that will provide a view of the glacier from above. Six of us are dropped on the shore, near the outlet of a small stream. We change out of the gumboots we use for our Zodiac transfers, and into our hiking boots. For the first time, I'm grateful to have my gaiters to keep the mud and gravel out of my boots. We leave our life jackets and gumboots in a pile and set out with Benja up the gentle slope, unaware that the greatest adventure of our journey lies just ahead.

ACTIVIST

On a cold, wet November morning, my friend David Johnstone escorted me to the bottom of the small road on the side of the mountain. I made my way to a scrum of reporters gathered under umbrellas in the cold, pelting rain. As I listened to others speak, a reporter put a lapel mic on my bright yellow-and-orange rain jacket. Another asked if I would hold his cell phone as I spoke. When my turn came, I spoke with defiance and pride, giving a short speech about the role of civil disobedience done in full respect of the rule of law, as a last resort in the face of an unjust law. I concluded by stating I was now going to turn and walk up that road to be the best citizen I could be. In an attempt to avoid the charge of flagrant defiance of the law, I carefully avoided stating my intent to be arrested. Thinking about it again now, my arrest was pretty flagrant even without those words. When I concluded my speech, there were cheers from the gathering crowd. The rain let up as I started up the hill to the police line. My friend Kathy Harrison took my arm and walked beside me. Soon, there were several of us linked arm in arm, walking up the hill in the rain, with supporters and reporters all around, walking with us.

About ten minutes later, we reached the police line. The RCMP were standing shoulder to shoulder. There was confusion as we tried to dash around them. Once again, afraid of drawing more serious charges, I was assiduous in not making physical contact with any of the police. I hadn't anticipated this move to block us from a peaceful arrest; I thought I would just walk through the yellow tape and be arrested. I was stymied. Our lines stood face to face, the tension building. Within a few minutes,

I was approached by a commanding officer with whom I'd developed a rapport in the preceding weeks – we'd each worked in our own realms to keep things as calm and peaceful as possible.

He warned me that if I didn't step down I would be arrested. I didn't step down. "So you're wanting to be arrested, is that right?" he said. "I am standing here willing to accept the consequences of my action," I replied. The police line parted; I stepped through and was immediately arrested. I raised my cuffed hands triumphantly over my head and stood tall with a big smile. There were hoots from supporters outside the line, and the commanding officer smiled and patted me on the shoulder. I sat with half a dozen women in the back of the patrol wagon. An officer asked if we were comfortable. I half expected them to offer us warm tea. I was shivering in my old rain jacket that was no longer waterproof. I was cold, but keenly aware of the difference between how I was being treated by the RCMP, and the much rougher experiences of my Indigenous friends.

After a drive of ten minutes or so, the patrol wagon delivered us to a parking lot near a playing field, where a temporary processing station was set up under a tent. I was chilled and disoriented, and don't remember much about the processing other than the fact that my court date was scheduled for my birthday, early in 2015. I was happy to see David waiting for me behind the fence – I hoped his car was close, and warm. As I started to walk towards him, someone handed me a phone and said, "Jo-Ann Roberts wants to interview you." At the time, I didn't know who Jo-Ann was, but I later learned that she was the host of *All Points West*, a popular afternoon CBC radio show out of Victoria. As I did the live interview with Jo-Ann, I paced around the field trying to warm up. What neither Jo-Ann nor I knew at the time was that we would meet in person a few months later, when both of us would be Green Party candidates in the 2015 federal election.

Many of us were arrested that day, including my friend Kevin Washbrook, who I met when we were both arrested blocking the coal train on the tracks in White Rock. In the days that followed, a ritual developed in which groups would gather at the bottom of the road, give speeches, and walk up to be arrested. As the days went on and teachers, religious leaders, and other groups made the walk, we gained increasing public support. I visited the protest site every day and tried to be there to witness and support those being arrested. I did an evening shift at the

Burnaby police station where arrestees were held for processing. We were there to greet protesters as they were released, providing granola bars and blankets, making sure everyone had a ride to shelter. On the mountain, a group of First Nations women lit a sacred fire behind the police line.

One day, I was standing at the yellow tape, helping maintain a presence. Three Indigenous women approached me from behind the line and escorted me to the sacred fire. I sat visiting with them for a while and when I rose to leave, the women rose and walked with me. As they escorted me back to the police-defined circumference, the women formed a circle around me and started drumming, dancing, and singing the Women's Warrior Song. I cried – this time tears of solidarity. I was in court again on the Friday when a group of First Nations leaders were arrested, garnering tremendous publicity and respect. I suspect Kinder Morgan couldn't wait to get their work done so they could get off the mountain and stop the flood of bad press.

On another day – a cold, rainy one – with a rainproof notepad, an umbrella and a borrowed GPS, I mapped the perimeter demarcated with yellow tape by the RCMP. Our lawyer had been tipped that the company might have had their coordinates wrong in their application for the injunction, and he asked me to check. I had to stand many minutes at each point, waiting for enough satellites positioned to provide sufficiently accurate information. These delays gave Trans Mountain ample opportunity to appreciate that we were on to their mistake. In the end, my data wasn't needed in court because the company came clean about the error in their application for an injunction. The placement of the police perimeter was about one hundred feet south of the location for which the judge had granted the injunction. Those of us arrested had been instructed to appear for sentencing, but it was all thrown out because none of us had actually violated the court order.

It was clear that when Kinder Morgan sued the five of us, what they were really after was the injunction to keep protestors off the mountain. They could only get this injunction by demonstrating to the court that our presence was costing them money, hence the threat they were coming after us for $5.6 million. This claim against us was without any merit whatsoever. Nevertheless, to get out from under the pressure of the lawsuit and to get on with our lives, four of us asked our lawyers to return to court and have the case discontinued, with no contingencies. Trans Mountain filed a public notice of discontinuance and the case is done, but the fight continues. The Canadian federal government and the government of the Province of Alberta continue to aggressively push the project, while growing numbers of Canadians and supporters from around the world continue to protest.

As I tell the story of my arrest, I think of the thousands of other people who have been arrested fighting fossil fuel projects – arrests that are often less gentle than my experience, and more consequential. Each one of these people has their own story of what brought them to this point, their experience of taking bold action, and the impacts on their lives. I'm grateful to each one.

I'd been in the local news all that fall, but my 21 November arrest and speech about civil disobedience made the national news. Within a week, I received an invitation from Elizabeth May, leader of the Green Party of Canada, to run as a Green candidate in the 2015 federal election. Hope was in the air and my ego felt the tug of being the chosen one. A hero was inviting me to do hero stuff side by side with her. By 29 November, I had agreed to run. At the time, I felt a strange mix of excitement and dread, reminiscent of plunging into Class IV rapids on the Chattooga River in an open canoe. Ten months later, standing on the metaphorical shore, soaking wet and bedraggled, I was gazing at a smashed canoe, knowing without a doubt that I was better suited to running river rapids than running in an election. I learned how the Cheaters have broken our political system and how the Green vote has been suppressed. And although I also learned that the Green Party isn't perfect, I know that if we are to address climate change, we need more Green voices in government.

EXPEDITION

It feels great to be moving. We're a small group trailing behind Benja like ducklings. I'm soon lost in my own thoughts as we hike on the west side of the ridge, out of sight of the ship and isolated from the other two landing parties. Looking west I can see more of the landscape than on any previous landing. I notice I am smiling. I'm feeling more intimately immersed in the wilderness than was possible on the ship or with the whole group on a beach landing. I'm happy to be here, happy to be healthy and taking joy in hiking. I want to walk for hours, but after only ten minutes, Risa calls for a photo stop. I resist, but soon I see the awesomeness of her call and pull out my camera, too. We've come to a saddle with a spectacular outlook across the fjord. In the distance, looking like ants, I see the largest landing party, strung out in single file, traversing the glacier. From this distance they look perilously close to the calving front. We have gained perhaps one hundred and fifty feet of elevation. Below us and slightly closer to the glacier is the stationary party.

The bay is full of ice – a mix of bergy bits and flat remnants from the fast ice, which not too long ago made this bay a fine place for a polar bear to stroll. A big, fat bearded seal lounges on a flat piece of ice drifting in the centre of the bay. Across the bay, a large mountain covered in patches of snow looms up out of the eastern shore. The sky is littered with clouds. In the still, black water, the reflections of snow and clouds mingle with the bergy bits. The effect is stunning, but I'm grateful when we start moving again.

We have resumed hiking for less than five minutes when Benja gets a call on his radio. We all hear Captain Joe's voice, "Benja, is Justin with you?" There are several minutes of trying to track down Justin. We have a strict system of signing on and off the ship so everyone is accounted for at all times. Eventually, Justin is found napping in his cabin. We continue our hike. Within a minute, we hear the captain on the radio again, "There is a bear approaching along the western shore." Western shore? *We* are on the western shore. We scramble back to the saddle, where we get a view back up the coast. Beyond the little stream where we left our gumboots and life jackets, I think I see the bear! It's a small yellow dot in the distance. I don't have a long lens on my camera, but I click away hoping an enlargement will document the adventure. Then, off to the right, I notice another yellow dot, this one closer to the shore and moving towards us. Click.

The first yellow dot I learn later was a reindeer, but the second yellow dot is now clearly a polar bear, becoming more distinct by the minute. It approaches the stream, enters the water, and emerges near where we left our stuff. It continues to approach. I've hiked in grizzly country and in a situation like this no self-respecting grizzly bear would continue to approach a group of half a dozen people. But the polar bear continues its steady pace towards us.

My excitement is morphing into fear. It hits me that twenty-one-year-old Benja from Patagonia, on his first trip to the Arctic, may be well trained, but he isn't experienced with polar bears. Has he misjudged our safety? How long would it take that hungry bear to reach us if he decided to run towards us? Just as I'm feeling the need to act, I see Sarah standing among us. She has climbed up the side of the ridge from the stationary landing on the beach to join us on the saddle.

Suddenly, the radio cackles again, "Evacuate, now!" We scramble quickly down the side of the moraine, down a scree slope and over patches of snow, towards the water. I look out over the bay and see two Zodiacs zooming at full speed towards the shore below us. I'm one of the first to reach the shore. I leap into a Zodiac and immediately start encouraging others to hurry up. Not everyone is sharing my fear. Some are diligently washing their boots before boarding the Zodiac, as Captain Joe trained us. Others from the shore party are carefully packing away their gear – although that changes quickly with a shout from Sarah.

Someone passes me my life jacket. Captain Joe and Ludo had waited until the bear passed our drop-off point, zoomed in to pick up our gear, and then rushed over to evacuate us. I look up and my heart stops: I see the bear appear on the ridge just as we're pushing off from shore. The bear scrambles over the edge and then toboggans on its belly down a large patch of snow. In no time at all, he is on the shore we have just left.

There is a lot of excitement, but Captain Joe, who is piloting our Zodiac, shushes us. For the next ten minutes or so, we quietly putter up the coast, watching the bear as he watches us. Not wanting to miss this photo opportunity, and not being an experienced photographer, I had switched my camera to "auto." Unfortunately, now my camera is auto-focusing on everything but the bear. I'm clicking like mad, trying to compose shots with the bear positioned where the camera wants to focus. Insanity! Hailey gently puts her hand on my arm and encourages me to put down my camera. I breathe deeply and at once I feel connected to the bear.

With the grace of a dancer he walks the shore – every muscle and every joint is connected in a single, smooth motion. In movement, he is strong and free. He navigates the shore, in and out of the water, now at the bottom of a rock face, moving north, away from the glacier, pausing now and then to sniff the air and peer at us. I breathe. I'm in awe. Where the ridge slopes down near sea level, not far from where we started our hike, the bear climbs and circles back, as though to continue towards the glacier. On top of the ridge, he sits and watches until we leave.

The mood on the ship is subdued. After the flush of sharing the story of our polar bear encounter with the others and reviewing our photos, the experience subsided into the surrealism of this entire journey. No one has mentioned how differently things might have played out if the captain hadn't been vigilant and spotted the bear as it approached from a distance along the western shore. To the few of us sitting around the table looking at photos, I express the concern I felt standing on the knoll watching the bear approach and then seeing him appear on the ridge just as we pushed off from shore. It seems I was the only one – at least among us "participants" – that felt these things, this alertness to risk.

Among my many good fortunes, I'm not unduly anxious. Nor do I feel the need to make the story any more dramatic than it was, to create excitement above and beyond the genuine thrill we all experienced by the encounter with the polar bear. I'm uncomfortable about the group's dismissiveness of the risk. I recall feeling similarly in the Zodiac when the six of us were momentarily trapped in the sea ice. But why do I feel this way? I agree we are in good hands and I didn't feel any real fear in either instance. Perhaps I'm interpreting their lack of concern as a lack of deference to nature, a lack of reverence. These thoughts lead me to wonder whether a lack of reverence underlies our societal inaction on environmental degradation. On some deep level – have people lost respect for the power of nature? Is there a vague and abstract trust that we'll be fine? Deference to nature notwithstanding, I'm disappointed our hike was cut short. I long to walk the wild land.

On deck, I watch the flat rocks of the island of Akseløya turn purple with saxifrage as we approach. Someone spots a polar bear in the distance, but I don't see it. Looming ahead, as we round the island into the inner fjord, are some of the most dramatic geological formations I've ever seen. Sedimentary layers have been uplifted to be almost vertical, forming mountains that rise thousands of feet from the sea and then plunge and fold and swirl back down again. Moss, lichen, and the black of carboniferous layers glow in the golden light. Sarah says we can't land here because reindeer are calving on the beach at the base of the mountains. Wisps of fog and clouds hide the peaks. Looking at the layers of buried carbon from extinct species, thinking of blue whales and polar bears, species that may soon face extinction, the history and the future of life on Earth collapse into this moment, and I feel it as the weight of a black hole.

ON ENERGY AND LIFE

In the mid-Arctic ridge, about halfway between Svalbard and Norway, lies a deep-sea alkaline hydrothermal vent named Loki's Castle, after the Norse god of fire and trickery. In 2014, a group of microorganisms were discovered living at Loki's Castle. These organisms, some named for Norse gods, are known only from the sequences of their DNA. No one has ever seen them.

Alkaline hydrothermal vents are distinct from the "black smokers" that you might have heard about. At alkaline vents, proton (pH) gradients form as a consequence of physical and chemical processes. Perhaps not coincidentally, proton gradients are the most fundamental way life stores its energy. Like a waterwheel capturing the energy of flowing water and using it to do work (such as grinding grain), protons flow down a gradient across a membrane and a molecular turbine captures some of that energy and makes ATP.

Energy is at the core of our origin story. Indeed, energy may come to define our whole story. While there is much we still don't know about our most ancient beginnings, the *geo*chemistry at alkaline hydrothermal vents may have gradually evolved into the *bio*chemistry of life. In his book *The Vital Question*, British biochemist Nick Lane tells a compelling story of how this could have happened.

In its most skeletal rendering, the story goes like this: Through cracks in the earth's crust, seawater seeps deep into the rocks, sometimes encountering the heat and minerals of the earth's mantle, including olivine. Olivine transforms into the more oxidized mineral serpentine, releasing hydrogen gas. Warmed by its encounter with the hot mantle, the water rises again, now stripped of protons and loaded with hydrogen. Chimneys of calcium carbonate form around the rising water, creating a proton gradient across the thin and perforated walls of the chimneys. The gradient is stored energy – like water behind a damn.

The proton gradients across the membranes of modern cells are typically about the same size as the gradients found in alkaline vents. The parallel begs us to imagine rudimentary molecular machines incidentally harnessing the gradient and building an ATP-like molecule. Ultimately, chains and rings of carbon combining in myriad ways – syntheses driven by ATP-like molecules generated by the proton gradient – could have led to copying machines and proto-cells.

Perhaps, as human birth is marked by a release from intimate dependence, the birth of life is marked by release from dependence on the vents. We can imagine that when cells achieved a means to make their own proton gradients, the umbilical cord between cells and rocks was severed.

While the boundary between life and non-life is fuzzy, there comes a point at which we can unambiguously say, "This thing is alive." The next big step was also about energy: simple cells became complex cells (and ultimately complex life) through the evolutionary invention of mitochondria.

For over a billion years, life on Earth was much like bacteria and archaea – biochemically interesting, but not much to look at. Then, around 2.7 billion years ago, an archaeum engulfed a bacterium. The union survived and together they evolved into a single, complex cell – each original cell gave up some functions as the cooperative became streamlined and energy efficient. Eventually, the bacterium became what we know as the mitochondrion.

Lane suggests the new energy efficiency freed cells from constraints that had kept them small and simple. Now they had the freedom to develop a dynamic cytoskeleton, an endomembrane system, cilia, a nucleus, and sexual reproduction. Arising from this lineage of complex cells, possibly triggered by the discovery of sexual reproduction, the magnificence of complex multicellular life blossomed like a daisy into diverse lineages, the ancestors of glorious beings – arctic terns, bearded seals, and lichens.

Complex life blows my mind. To witness the grace of a long-limbed polar bear in motion, to feel the emotional tug of the songs of a bearded seal, to travel alongside a family of blue whales, to look at snow algae through the microscope – these are spiritual experiences akin to the most profound experience of human-made art.

In our story so far, some consider the emergence of consciousness to be the final grand leap. I wonder if the climactic grand leap in the dance of energy and life might have come when the most complex of the complex species discovered fossil fuels – carbon fixed into complex organic molecules by life that lived eons ago. The discovery of this energy source powered the development of industrialized civilization and simultaneously transformed Earth's atmosphere. Will our dance with energy resolve with a beautiful pirouette and a surprising denouement?

EXPEDITION

This morning, our landing is on the beach in front of Recherchebreen. Here the retreating glacier has dumped huge piles of sand and then made a rapid retreat, leaving an ice-filled lagoon between the sandy beach of our landing and its present active face. Bergy bits drift in a large circle in the lagoon, revealing the current that is actively undermining the face and causing a constant cascade of ice. The lagoon reflects the intense blue of the sky; the water sparkles with sunlight. There are polar bear footprints in the sand – but not too fresh. Again, we spread ourselves over all available terrain.

After mentioning climate activism in my ten-minute project talk, I've been having lots of conversations about climate change. As a result, I've been asked to give an impromptu talk on climate science to the group after dinner this evening. I have lots of material on my laptop so putting together some visuals will be easy, but I am occupied with thinking about what to cover and how to present it. As it turns out, this evening's talk is also on Adam's mind. He does a video interview with me on climate change with the collapsing glacier as a backdrop.

Emma is in hip waders in the lagoon, tugging ice into position. On a previous expedition, Sarah found the carcass of a young polar bear that had apparently starved to death at the northern tip of Spitsbergen. She returned with a small group and they delivered the carcass to the lab of artist Michael Günzburger. Michael carefully cleaned and oiled the fur and made a print of the bear on four large sheets of paper. Emma has brought this print on our trip, and at several of our landings the bear has been repatriated. When we were moored to the ice floe, four artists assembled the four sheets and crouched behind them to walk the bear across the ice, while Adam shot video of the exercise. Now Emma carries the print of the emaciated polar bear out piece by piece until the four sheets are positioned on a slab of ice floating in the lagoon.

After assisting Emma, I climb a small hill, a glacial moraine, where I sit, surveying the strange panorama of artists at work. Beth is interviewing Lucy about scars and tattoos. Cara is interviewing a small group in turns about times when they were lost. Bee sits sketching. Deidre is meditating. M is doing yoga. Robert is exploring the mud. Susan is making a video recording of the drifting ice. Justin is taking photographs of Anna dressed in an extravagant gown, lounging on an ice floe. Brandy is dancing her mournful polar bear dance in a protected spot beside a small knoll. Rachael is recording the sounds of melting ice. And Emma photographs the repatriated bear.

"for a short time, we felt like a gang of strange gods."
– Rachael Dease, posted to Facebook on our return home

Sitting on the knoll, I wonder: which projects will come to fruition? What will the projects contribute? Who will be influenced? Much of what I am seeing perplexes and amuses me. I lack the knowledge or the vision to see where the work is going. In Oslo, en route to Longyearbyen, I saw two works by Ai Weiwei at the Astrup Fearnley Museum of Modern Art, both inspired by his time in Lesbos, when Syrian refugees were arriving across the sea. "Tyres" consists of piles of lifebuoys, all sculpted from marble, like Greek statues. The walls of the room are papered with "Odyssey": rows of black-and-white images reminiscent of the decorations on a Greek vase, images of global refugee migrations – camps and processions, borders and barbed wire. Both works are at once beautiful and disturbing political commentary on a world on the threshold of massive migrations driven by climate change. Had I seen but not recognized Ai Weiwei lying on a pebble beach in Lesbos, in the pose of the now iconic image of the drowned Syrian child, Aylan Kurdi, would I have dismissed Ai as crass or frivolous? It seemed silly when four artists "walked" the polar bear print around the ice floe while a fifth made a video recording. Yet, in a few months I will see Adam's slow-motion video of this walk and be moved more deeply than by any photographs of the living bear encountered on our hike. The unedited footage begins with a lot of shuffling about, getting organized on deck – a fun "home movie" for our troupe of strange gods. The artists descend the gangplank and organize themselves behind the four quadrants of the bear. It takes a few attempts and I am caught off guard when suddenly an emaciated bear is lumbering across the ice floe. I felt nothing beyond amusement when watching the action in real time, but the eerie slow-motion animation elicits a deep sadness. It grows in me as I contemplate the care with which the carcass was moved, oiled, and printed, the artists who conceived the return of the "bear" to the sea ice, and of course, the bear that died of starvation. Sometimes, it takes an unusual and provocative shift to knock us out of a flat response to a pervasive iconic image, like the polar bear. It occurs to me that the risks involved in experimenting with unusual and provocative shifts are akin to the risks at the leading edges of science. Recalling the intuition I developed as a cell biologist, I appreciate the years of study that underlie the artists' sense of which risks might be worth taking.

As I scan the scene before me and note new activities, I wonder if some projects have been abandoned; a few of the artists seem to be floundering or searching. The prospects for my own watermelon snow project are not looking good. This is something else that art and science have in common: not everything we do succeeds.

I pick up a handful of gravel from the moraine where I am sitting. It is a reminder that I am part of a nature that includes not only microbes and polar bears, but also the rocks and water that gave birth to life. Under the bluest sky imaginable, the water is sparkling to out-sparkle any water anywhere, and the ice is the shiniest, most glistening ice in the world. The day seems to be celebrating. Busy at their tasks, our strange gang of humble gods is each, in their way, seeking meaning. I am awash with that most esteemed religious experience, love.

ON LITTLE CELLS DOING BIG THINGS

There is another lineage of microbes in the history of life on Earth that were truly god-like in their actions. The story goes like this: In the early days of life on Earth, there was very little oxygen in the atmosphere, and that was a good thing because for early life oxygen was a poison. Sometime around three billion years ago, the lineage known as the cyanobacteria discovered photosynthesis. When photons strike a molecular machine that serves as an antenna, electrons are catapulted to high-energy states (recall the little kid on the trampoline). Cyanobacteria discovered ways to buffer the fall of the electrons and use the energy to pump protons across a membrane, thus converting the energy of light into a handy proton gradient from which they already knew how to make ATP.

The cyanobacteria subsequently discovered that by splitting water, they had an endless supply of juicy high-energy electrons to feed the process. Life was good and the nasty waste product, oxygen, was dumped into the environment.

For a long time, the production of this pollutant wasn't a problem because there were lots of sinks to soak up the oxygen – iron, for example, rusting to red iron oxides. But eventually the sinks filled and oxygen began to accumulate in the atmosphere.

Now at this time, methane was abundant in the atmosphere, and, being a powerful greenhouse gas, methane was keeping the earth warm. When oxygen reacted with the methane, carbon dioxide, a much less potent greenhouse gas, was produced, and the earth began to cool. The earth cooled so dramatically it entered a global ice age known as Snowball

Earth (although some scientists think it was probably more like slush ball Earth, with liquid water remaining near the equator).

And so it was that the discovery by cyanobacteria of an awesome new way to make a proton gradient ended up poisoning the atmosphere and triggering massive climate change. This was likely the first mass extinction of life on Earth. Some lineages, including the cyanobacteria, squeaked through. We have no idea what evolutionary inventions might have been lost, but life survived. The cyanobacteria couldn't have known the consequences of their discovery, nor could they have changed course had they known.

Now we are the species remodelling the planet by dumping carbon dioxide, the waste product of our energy consumption, into the atmosphere. We know what we're doing and it's within our abilities to change course.

The "strange gods" of this expedition are humble seekers. In contrast, many of our politicians and multinational CEOs are a little like Greek gods, with power that is for the most part uncoupled from wisdom. They excel at manipulation and conniving to get what they want, yet rarely do they see the emptiness and folly of their desires. Will our god-like species find a way to unite power with wisdom?

EXPEDITION

We return to the *Antigua* for lunch. As I slide in beside Brett, he pulls a book from the shelf behind our seat. Raising both eyebrows, he holds it up so I can see the cover. It looks like a Ladybird book, the title in a 1930s typeface: *Last Chance to See*. Brett passes me the book and says, as though to a young child, "See how nicely the Komodo dragon and the river dolphin are playing together." I take the book, noting that it is co-authored by Douglas Adams, author of many beloved science fiction books, including *The Hitchhiker's Guide to the Galaxy*. When the dolphins in *Hitchhiker's Guide* escape an Earth that is about to be destroyed, their last message to the humans is: "So long, and thanks for all the fish." When my son walked across the stage for high school graduation, his message to us all was: "So long, and thanks for all the fish." Douglas Adams was a favourite in our household.

And yet, as I look at the eerily peaceful storybook depiction of a Yangtze River dolphin, I feel sick to my stomach. The dolphin in question is now extinct. I flip through the book and see science infused with Adams's quirky humour. A world tour to see species on the cusp of extinction – to raise awareness, but also, I suspect, because it was something the authors wanted to do. The book was published in 1990. Does this make it okay in the way that, if one is so inclined, it can be easier to forgive an old man his misogyny? I am not in a forgiving mood. I am repulsed by the book – not by the authors or by a text I haven't read, but by the extinctions we are causing, and by what has since become a thing: extinction tourism. And now I feel called out – by my own thoughts, by Brett handing me this book.

Here I am. Here we are. I close the book and hand it back to Brett, who has been watching all of this play out on my face. He smiles and says softly, "I knew you'd understand." He gently reshelves the book. Has he just executed a small and personal act of art?

While we eat lunch, the crew pulls anchor and takes us a short distance to Kapp Toscane. Our afternoon landing will be at Hvitfiskstranda, "white whale beach," the site of a whaling camp from the 1930s where belugas were butchered for their meat.

On the beach are piles of bleached white bones. The skulls are close to the size of human skulls, and I can't shake images of the piles of human skulls assembled by the Khmer Rouge in Cambodia. I walk the beach, photographing the piles of bones. Using DNA from two beluga whales that died in the Vancouver Aquarium in 2016, my colleague Steve Jones and his collaborators sequenced the beluga genome. This was a tremendous technical accomplishment and has supplied us with a vast store of data about the genome and its expression in various tissues of the whale. In a different world, this information might one day be useful in conservation efforts. With great sadness, I view this accomplishment much as I view the more grandiose proposals for geoengineering – such projects miss the point. They can't substitute for radical and immediate reductions in our GHG emissions, without which action we'll lose the belugas, whether or not we know the sequence of their genome.

Once again we're crowded into the salon. I'm nervous. At dinner Sarah had reminded everyone that tonight would be the "climate change debate." Debate? Surely this isn't going to be a debate. Climate change is an emotional topic and when I began this work, deniers and would-be deniers have challenged me with science-sounding claims, usually based on a nugget of fact. It has been a while since anyone has accused me of being part of a global conspiracy, but it's still common for people to lash out with random objections. I suspect such people are lashing out in self-defence, not yet ready to face the responsibility that comes with knowing the truth. I get it. The data freaks me out, too. I'll talk science, not politics, and yet, I know that how I am perceived will influence how the message is received.

I'm nervous this evening because I'm about to talk about data that moves me to the core. Having previously established my science cred with this crowd helps, but climate science is political. People take it personally. My plan is to bring the focus fully into the realm of science in order to engage people who might not like the political consequences of the data. This is comfortable territory for me – I'm well versed in the limits of various data sets, the range of possible interpretations, limits to extrapolating from paleo-climate data, the use and limits of models. In my experience, even many people who are concerned about climate change have little knowledge of the actual data. When people see the data for the first time, they often become alarmed. I think this is an appropriate response. I proceed with strength because I believe a realistic understanding of the situation is necessary to drive appropriate action.

What does a gang of strange gods need to know about global warming and climate change? I pare it down to the most fundamental, essential data. I start with global warming and Ed Hawkins's animated spiral plot – a visualization of average monthly global temperature anomalies around a circle, one round per year. As the years pile up, at first there is a tight ring near the centre, but then the temperature begins to spiral out. These data are calculated global averages and they show clearly how the earth has shifted out of energy balance and is warming at an accelerating rate.

For another perspective, I show an animated world map from NASA that uses a heat map (a colour-coded representation of temperature anomalies in which the intensity of red corresponds to the amount of warming, and blue to cooling) to present the global distribution of temperature anomalies in rolling five-year averages. The dramatic temperature increase in the Arctic is arresting.

I point out the cooling spot just off of Greenland, a consequence of a lens of cold fresh water from the melting Greenland ice sheet. Being fresh, the lens floats on top of the denser salt water underneath and slows the normal sinking of cold Arctic water, with serious consequences for ocean circulation.

I explain the greenhouse effect and then show the Keeling Curve, direct daily measurements of atmospheric carbon dioxide since 1958. The steady rise of the annual seasonal oscillation is dramatic. I point out the accelerating rate of accumulation – an acceleration that hasn't abated in spite of the numerous good news stories about the phasing out of coal, the blossoming of the solar industry, innovative agricultural practices, and so on.

The room is quiet. I see tears in the eyes of an artist near the front and wonder for a moment whether I should stop here. For those who have focused on the good news stories, of which there are many, it can come as a shock to see that our emissions are continuing to accelerate. I continue.

Scientists have taken deep cores in Arctic and Antarctic ice sheets and measured carbon dioxide concentrations in air bubbles trapped in the ice going back 800,000 years. I show these data and point out the ragged oscillations that correspond to the ice ages. I show how rises in carbon dioxide and temperature are rapid and steep, whereas the falls are more ragged and slower. This is because the increases in carbon dioxide and temperature are hastened by positive feedback loops. These are the same data I had walked alongside in Dresden. I point out how sea level rise lags significantly behind carbon dioxide and temperature. It takes a lot of energy (and therefore time) to melt ice. I show how to ballpark the sea level rise we can expect as a result of the warming we have already experienced. I explain how the earlier slopes give a hint of how quickly it's likely to happen. We walk through a "back of the envelope" estimate. It isn't hard to understand, everyone gets it.

I rush through the chemistry of dissolving carbon dioxide in seawater, the dramatic impacts of warming and acidification that we're already seeing on life in the ocean. I barely mention the risk of melting the methane hydrates on the coastal shelves and in permafrost, which would cause a release of methane that would substantially amplify the warming we're already experiencing. In recent years, methane levels have begun to rise, but this is due to the activity of microbes in melting tundra and fugitive methane from fracking. Thankfully, we haven't yet crossed the tipping point of releasing the massive stores of frozen methane. Crossing this tipping point would trigger a cascade of tipping points, including the loss of all ice sheets, resulting in approximately seventy metres of sea level rise, although that would likely take several hundred years.

I need to stop soon. People near the front look stunned. Risa is staring blankly ahead, eyes wide, lips parted. I can hear restless movements in the back of the salon. I want to stop while everyone is still sufficiently engaged to process and question. I panic a little and my heart starts racing; I need to bring it home before I lose them. I pause and make eye contact with Risa. Rachael. Brett. Hailey. Each nods and I go on: The rapid warming of the Arctic means that the large temperature differential that plays an important role in establishing climate is weakened. This and a warmer atmosphere carrying more water is why we're seeing more severe weather – stronger storms, hotter wild fires, catastrophic floods, and prolonged droughts.

The lens of cold fresh water off Greenland is contributing to a weakening of the critically important major Atlantic meridional overturning circulation (AMOC). If AMOC stalls, the implications are enormous, including extremely cold winters in Europe, hotter summers and extended droughts in Africa, and more-rapid sea level rise for the eastern US. We're facing loss of species, especially in the oceans, but also on land, as climatic regions shift faster than species can migrate or adapt. (So far, the accelerated rate of extinctions is due to habitat fragmentation and pollution. Climate-related extinctions are just beginning.) Related to all of these things, we're already seeing increased famine, human migration, and war. We're facing radical changes in our weather systems, with severe impacts on human civilization. It's happening now and it will continue to get worse. How fast it gets worse and how bad it gets is up to us.

I pause for emphasis: *There is a yawning chasm of difference between how bad things will get if we continue business-as-usual and how bad they will be if we get off fossil fuels as soon as possible.* As I say the words, I wonder to myself whether the chasm is really still yawning. I don't emphasize that the logical conclusion from the data I've just presented is that whatever we do or don't do now, we're already locked in for serious climate chaos. There will be major upheavals in civilization as we know it. I don't have the courage to share that the continuing acceleration of carbon dioxide accumulation and the state of political discourse has me on the verge of tears almost every day.

I've presented the problem and its urgency. I've connected the dots from fossil fuels to carbon dioxide to consequences that affect us all. What comes next is important, but my confidence flags. People always want to know what to do. Sometimes, the awareness of all that I could be doing can weigh me down to the point of not being able to act at all. I refuse to be prescriptive – individual responses to different solutions vary dramatically. And that is okay because climate change is a complex problem – it requires us to pull together, towards the same goals, but not necessarily doing the same things. My approach is to open the floor at this point and allow solutions to emerge, as they always do.

After a moment of quiet, there is an angry voice from the back corner of the upper table. Jesus is a small man in his early sixties. He is a proud

Basque and a painter of landscapes. Tonight, his English is more heavily accented than usual, and at first, I have a difficult time understanding why he's so upset.

Then the word "hypocrite" comes through loud and clear. In a quivering voice he says something like: "We are all hypocrites for sitting here talking about the climate because we've all made the trip here and are being ferried around Svalbard mostly by diesel. We are a big part of the problem and if we really cared we would have stayed home and recycled." I suppress the urge to ask Jesus if he is suggesting that only those who opt out of a system that is so utterly dependent on and entwined with fossil fuels can talk about climate change. "Hypocrite" is a common charge I hear from those who would prefer that none of us talk about climate change. It is a statement of denial. I wonder whether his anger is coming from guilt, or perhaps he fears that the solutions won't allow him to live the life he aspires to – this expedition, for example.

I *had* thought long and hard about the carbon cost of my participation in this expedition. My own carbon footprint is never far from my mind. I'm committed to working hard to leverage my experience here into total reductions in emissions that trivialize my personal emissions. While I know this is possible, it won't be easy. Certainly, I can't justify this level of emissions very often – perhaps never again. This doesn't feel like sacrifice to me. It feels like an opportunity to slow down, to enjoy anticipation, to cherish and savour every local adventure. I feel this way about all of the changes I've made as I continue in my efforts to construct a life and a community in harmony with the rest of nature. My life is richer, not poorer.

I've stayed out of the "hypocrite" discussion and didn't really pay attention as some of the others went back and forth with Jesus. Now, people have transitioned into talking about what we can do.

The group talks for a while about the actions we can take as individuals and consumers, offering one another suggestions that eventually cover pretty much the full spectrum: fly less, drive less, use public transit, walk, bike, eat local and low on the food chain, buy less, buy used, compost, reuse, repurpose, avoid plastic, change your light bulbs, wash your clothes in cold water, hang to dry, avoid packaging, and divest from fossil fuel companies and the banks that fund them.

I'm relieved when Cara offers, "These individual actions are necessary, but not sufficient." Hailey states the fact that "There are too many humans." Jessamyn has this one: "Providing education and opportunities for women is key to reducing population." We talk about how lifestyle changes do bring down our communal carbon footprint, but more importantly, they stir people to higher levels of engagement.

It feels good to listen. My talk has bumped up the sense of urgency for this gang of intelligent people who already have the values and knowledge to pull in the direction of a post-carbon world. I regret that there wasn't more time to talk about the carbon costs of manufacturing, refrigerants, building materials, and industrial agriculture. I would have liked to discuss the role of building local community, and reconnecting with nature. There was not nearly enough time to take the conversation into deeper issues of democracy, neo-colonialism, de-growth, social inequality. There are many dots to connect. Wholesale system changes that need to be made.

The conversations have fragmented and I pull us back together for a wrap-up. I emphasize that one of the most important things we can do is to talk about climate change. By working to reduce our own personal footprints, we inspire and motivate others to action, both personal and political. I emphasize that individual behavioural change, however diligent and widespread, isn't enough. Nor is it necessarily something we should expect from everyone. It is only with regulatory changes, new policies, and cultural shifts that we can build a society where low carbon choices are the easy, appealing choices. If we don't take back the power, corporations will continue to dictate environmental regulations and policy that favours pollution on a scale that wipes out all of the individual and community good we might do – pollution in service of enriching the rich.

Overall, the evening went well and the conversations will continue for the remainder of our journey and beyond. But in my heart, I know I've missed something important. I think of my own burnout and depression, Jesus's anger, the tears welling in the eyes of some listeners as I spoke, and I realize, in failing to address the emotional impacts of the science, I have failed in the deepest way.

ON POLITICIANS AND CLIMATE CHANGE

After my brief experience in politics, I've become more cautious about attributing motives to politicians. But, even with buckets of caution and goodwill, it's very difficult to see the actions of some politicians in a positive light. They may be misguided, but the information is readily available and there is a serious failure in leadership on the part of any politician today who denies climate change or expresses concern but fails to act in robust and serious ways.

Much has been written about how the fossil fuel industry (and others) have captured democratic institutions in Canada and the US, and "manufactured consent" for their projects. What genuinely perplexes me is how so many politicians who seem like good people can be twisted into alignment with this nasty industry. It keeps me up at night. I don't believe anyone is threatening to kidnap and torture their children, and I can't fathom the mind that would lead one to exchange personal wealth or power or prestige for global warming, even if they believe their families will be sheltered by their wealth. Unless, perhaps, they don't fully understand what is happening, which, I suppose, is possible.

At the end of the day, politicians work for us. We hire them with our votes and with our votes they get to keep their jobs. The failure of our politicians is our failure. In her TED talk, climate scientist Katharine Hayhoe says that the most important action we can take is to talk about climate change. I think that she is right. The more of us who understand the urgency, the more likely we are to hire political leaders willing to pull with us instead of against us. Participatory democracy requires participation.

EXPEDITION

At breakfast this morning, Risa is excitedly sharing the news of connecting to the Internet. When she heard a "ding" from Susan's phone in the night, Risa astutely realized we were picking up a signal as we passed Longyearbyen en route up the fjord. She enthusiastically shares how she leapt out of bed and went upstairs to connect with the world while the rest of us slept. Others start talking about wanting news of the world. I wonder if one of the reasons I find solace in wilderness is that I cherish being disconnected from the world. I'm in no rush for news; I'm fully absorbed by our journey.

When I step on deck, I find we are once again at anchor in front of a glacier, our last glacier, Nordenskiöldbreen. (When did I start having breakfast before stepping on deck?) We're at one extreme edge of the glacier, where a low tongue of ice rests on rock and feeds several small waterfalls. Because the ice rests on land and isn't undercut by the sea, it isn't calving. We're anchored close to shore, and I stand on deck watching as some of our gang are ferried ashore and scramble up and over the rocks onto the snow and ice. I record tranquil footage of the glacier with a gentle breeze on the water and an occasional gull flying by. Susan has set up her tripod on the deck; she captures video of the strange gods at play in colourful glory on the snow and ice. It's a short landing and soon we're on our way to Pyramiden.

For the first time on the trip, I'm not looking forward to our next landing. We're nearing the end of our journey, and I wish we could spend our remaining time close to nature. Instead, we're headed to a Russian ghost town in the process of being born again as a tourist destination. There is considerable interest in our group for visiting the site, but I've had my fill of human folly, and I'm reluctant to witness this particular example. We moor to the pier, and I join for the walk and to see the views from town, and also because, although repelled, I'm curious.

The story of Pyramiden is a Cold War story. Under the Svalbard Treaty, ratified in 1925, Norway has limited sovereignty over the demilitarized archipelago. Svalbard is visa-free and numerous countries are represented in the research community at Ny-Ålesund. Although the over forty signatories to the treaty have equal rights to engage in commercial activities, only Norway and Russia pursued the development of permanent settlements. Pyramiden was a Russian mining town run by a state-owned company. It's unclear to me whether its existence was ever self-sustaining or whether the coal mine was simply justification for the establishment of a Soviet town in a Western-world-dominated part of the Arctic. What is clear is that after the Second World War, Pyramiden became much more than a mining town. It became a showcase of the Soviet Union. There was a cultural centre with a plush auditorium, a large heated swimming pool, a gym, a basketball court, a community playground, a soccer field, an elementary school, a hospital, a cafeteria, apartment blocks to house over 1,000 people, and a spacious central town square covered in a luscious lawn and overseen by a bust of Lenin. Barge load after barge load of soil was brought in for the lawn and the greenhouses, where fresh produce was grown in the summer months. Life in Pyramiden was privileged. For fifty years, workers and their families, administrators and visitors, arrived by boat and by plane, bringing stuff to Pyramiden with every trip. Showcase as it was, the town was a financial drain on the mother country.

When the Soviet Union collapsed in 1991, things went quickly downhill in Pyramiden. Morale was already low when a tragic plane crash in 1996 killed 141 community leaders, workers, and children. In March 1998 the company made the decision to close the town, and before the summer sun was gone, everyone had been evacuated. All that was left was fifty years' worth of accumulated stuff, including an invasive grass inedible to the local reindeer. And because this is the Arctic, cold and dry, nature is slow to reclaim the land.

As we walk up the gravel road from the pier to town, past abandoned warehouses, industrial-looking buildings, and great piles of rusting metal parts, I'm agog at the setting. To the left of the road is a luscious wetland, on the opposite side of which rise jagged, snow-capped peaks. Ahead, a sign announces the town. The sign is a tower sitting on a four-foot-high base of stone blocks. The tower-sign is built in sections of parallel rust-red rods forming a narrow box, or cage, perhaps four feet tall, with the array of rods above forming a slightly smaller cage. Finally, at the top of the tower is a star. In front of the lowest and widest cage of red bars is a large, stylized, sky-blue, C-shaped surface with "Pyramiden" in large, white block letters, in Russian and in English. Here, in the middle of nowhere, there can be no doubt what town this is. The sign is a bold symbol of the pride that once lived here. I think of Robert branding the ice with "Mine."

The town stands at the top of a small valley surrounded by rugged mountains. To our right, its lower slopes entering the town, a giant, pyramid-shaped mountain defines this place and mesmerizes me with the colours of its striations. Clouds cover the sun, and the mountain broods. A covered rail track crawls up the side of the mountain to the mine entrance near the peak. From the boardwalk next to the playground I breathe in the view back down the valley, across the fjord to the sparkling and expansive Nordenskiöldbreen, but I choke on the stench of ammonia. Kittiwakes have taken over the town. Their nests crowd the windowsills of apartment blocks; there are nests on the swing sets, the jungle gym, and all along the wooden structures of elevated coal chutes – so many wonderful places to lay eggs out of reach of foxes and polar bears. Such a cacophony of squawks!

We continue up through town, past the apartment blocks surrounding the expansive lawn of the town square. After posing for photos with the bust of Lenin and peeking in the windows of the Cultural Centre, we continue up the valley beyond the town. A gentle road leads up to a ridge beyond which a small river flows around the northern flank of town to the wetlands below. Over a bridge and around a bend we find ourselves at a small shed built of glass bottles. The Glass House, set a little away from the centre of town, was the place to come to for a few drinks and maybe some dancing. On our walk back into town, there is a rangy-looking reindeer grazing near the road. He's mid-moult and still clad in shaggy bits of what was once a luxurious winter coat.

As we've wandered through town in our small groups, each with an alert guide with a rifle – a polar bear in town can approach quickly, blocked from sight by the many abandoned buildings – we have seen other groups of tourists poking about. Today all of the buildings are locked, but tomorrow morning some of us will return and a local guide will open doors to reveal an abandoned piano, crushed velvet seats in an auditorium, spilled reels of film, photos cut from magazines pinned to the walls of a bedroom, steel-frame bed askew, mattress propped against a wall. We return through the square and approach the newly renovated and open-for-business hotel. There is a small museum that is closed, but this afternoon the pub is open. It's crowded with tourists – mostly Norwegians – and we wait in line for a frothy glass of cold ale, which turns out to be the deliciously perfect thing at this moment. We spend a boisterous hour in the pub and then walk back to the ship.

As we walk along the pier to the *Antigua*, we see that Sasha, Jana, Alex, and Sylvi have prepared a surprise feast for us on the deck of the ship. There is a barbecue going, tables piled with food, and music playing. (Vegetarian fare includes skewers of barbecued dill pickles.) Soon, the tables of food are cleared away and there is dancing, with music that spans the generations. I enjoy the movement and relish that my back is free of pain. I like to dance with abandon – like no one is watching. But then I spot Risa's little 360 camera sitting on the deck, facing the dancers. Suddenly self-conscious, I leave the dancers and join a small group sitting on the deck, leaning against one of the Zodiacs. I realize I've landed in the middle of an intense personal conversation and politely drift away.

For a while, I am at the railing of the main deck sharing childhood stories with Emma. Then, I wander into the salon and discover it feels like a club. The portholes are shuttered and the skylight covered. A mirror ball spins. Brett is behind the bar serving as deejay. The vibe is very different from that out on the deck – and there are no cameras in evidence. I join Deidre and Jessamyn and we find the rhythm. Wait! Isn't that Carl Sagan's voice! And Stephen Hawking! I glance over at Brett and see him grinning as the recognition hits me. He's having fun with the two scientists, physicist and biologist, dancing in his club. It's strange to step back out onto the deck and into the sun. Now there is another dance party happening up on the dock. I notice the camera and refrain from joining (silly, I know). I enjoy more personal conversations with shipmates than in all the days of the preceding weeks combined – life stories are starting to emerge. One by one, the strange gods are becoming mortal humans.

We spend the night moored at the Pyramiden pier. In the morning some of our group make a second visit to the ghost town. Many remain behind; I'm not the only one disturbed by the human detritus that will linger for centuries. Or perhaps the detritus won't linger. The Arctic is unlikely to remain cold and dry.

EXPEDITION

This afternoon we made the short trip to Skansbukta for our final landing of the expedition. The *Antigua* is anchored in a quiet, ice-free bay on a long beach at the base of a mountain whose rugged rock cap looks like the ramparts of a castle. It towers over a broad skirt of eroding rock, which turns to scree at its angle of repose. We're deep in the fjord, and this bay has a particularly peaceful feeling. I think Sarah and Captain Joe have selected it as our final landing for that reason.

There is an old wooden shipwreck near the middle of the beach, and at the close end of the beach rail tracks go into the side of the mountain. Here is another abandoned mine, but this time the rocks scattered about are not black, but white. I recognize it as gypsum. The mine entrance is accessible and there is much talk about the cramped and difficult life of the miners. I think how much worse it must have been for the coal miners. Now, in places like West Virginia, in the US, we just blow the tops off the mountains and load up the coal. I walk to the far end of the beach. There is no wind where I stand, but as I contemplate a high waterfall that cascades through the ramparts, I see it blow gently to the right for a while, and then to the left. The water is at the mercy of mountain winds until it hits solid ground on the skirt of the mountain, where it disappears into the scree and flows underground, feeding the green and soggy moss at the base of the mountain.

I find a log and, wondering where on Earth it drifted from, I sit and watch the waterfall. Instead of returning to Longyearbyen in the morning, I want to go north again. I loved it all – the ice, the polar bear – and I feel I didn't appreciate it deeply enough when we were there. I was overwhelmed and overstimulated, and I had a sore back, and a cold, and it was all over too fast. I watch the waterfall suddenly fall straight and then shift to the left. I realize it isn't just the trip north that I want to repeat. I feel much the same about life. The waterfall blows more radically to the left. Down the beach, everyone is doing their thing much as they have done on every other beach. In some strange way, I haven't accepted that this is our last landing. My mind refuses to go forward and prepare for the coming days. I watch the waterfall slump into a straight fall, and I cast my mind back.

For the past decade I've been, perhaps, a bit manic with fear. When I finally understood the magnitude and urgency of global warming, I panicked. I felt a tremendous weight of moral responsibility to act, to join the climate justice movement and do everything in my power to help humanity change course. I gave it everything until I had nothing left to give. Yet, the situation remains urgent and some days it feels not much has changed, or that some things are changing, but much too slowly. Gradually, I've become aware that global warming will define not just the present, but the entirety of my remaining life.

When I started on this path, I believed that with a big push we would turn things around. That might have been true then, but it is too late for that now. These are the times of my life. How do I come to terms with such knowledge?

In her memoir, *In Gratitude*, Jenny Diski writes about dying of cancer. She quotes Beckett, from *From an Abandoned Work*: "I too shall cease and be as when I was not yet, only all over instead of in store." Diski goes on to write, "When I find myself trembling at the prospect of extinction, I can steady myself by thinking of the abyss that I've already experienced. Sometimes I can almost take a kindly, unhurried interest in my own extinction." In this very personal grief about her own imminent death, Diski writes of the abyss, the before and the after. This, I think, approaches what I've been writing towards: there is solace in the contemplation of evolutionary time.

> Imagine that you and some other humans are in a spaceship, roaming around in the universe, looking for a home. You land on a planet that proves to be ideal in every way. It has

deep forests and fleshy fruits and surging oceans and gentle rains and cavorting creatures and dappled sunlight and rich soil. Everything is perfect for human habitation, and everything is astonishingly beautiful.
– Ursula Goodenough, *The Sacred Depths of Nature*

With this passage, Goodenough is describing the gratitude of finding that we arrived on Earth "but a moment ago and found it to be perfect for us in every way. And then we came to understand that it is perfect because we arose from it and are part of it." There was life before we arrived; there will be life after we are gone. To be sure, we humans are hastening change and pushing things in a direction other than what might have been – perhaps not so different than has been done by other species before us.

I breathe and watch the water appear at the top of the ramparts and cascade down its short but spectacular life as a waterfall; the water bounces up briefly as it strikes the scree and then falls again and disappears underground. Only now do I see that this Arctic trip has been like a "celebration of life" for ice. I think of this new gang of mine, standing together on the deck of the *Antigua* listening to the bearded seals singing to one another under the fast ice of Raudfjorden. There was joy and celebration in our exclamations of surprise, laughter, and fellowship as we shared the astonishing experience of summer sea ice. Some of us shared sadness when we awoke to find ourselves tethered to a much smaller ice floe than we had played on the day before. We all delighted in the immensity of the glaciers, the ethereal sky-blue glow of some bergy bits, the tinkling sounds of a bay filled with ice from a crumbling glacier, the reverberating gunshot and splash of calving. Every day, we celebrated ice. And every day there was sorrow at how much a glacier had retreated, at the sight of a polar bear in distress.

Some of us arrived in the Arctic already mourning personal loss; others among us came here to do work exploring the various losses arising from colonialism, past and ongoing – devastating social inequality and environmental degradation. Grief was explicitly present in Brandy's polar bear dancing, Emma's polar bear print and her unravelling project, Rachael's fusions of death and science, Risa's focus on melting, Robert's critique of colonialism, and Susan's meditative photography of earth that once was ice. I thought I was here for snow algae, art, and adventure.

I stand and stretch, feeling I've made progress on solving a problem that I haven't quite defined. I stroll down the beach to the spot where others are putting on life jackets and preparing for Zodiac rides back to the *Antigua*.

We moored overnight in the quiet bay by the waterfall and it was a short trip this morning back to the dock at Longyearbyen, where we are now loading our piles of gear into the bowels of the bus, ready for the trip up the valley to the Coal Miners' Cabins. I grin and nod for Risa to check out the line waiting to give a farewell hug to Ludo.

Tonight, we are on our own for dinner (tomorrow will be a farewell banquet). I take my time and wander down the valley to the pub, where Jessamyn will be giving her promised workshop on comedy. We'd hoped to have the workshop on the ship, but there was never enough time. There is never enough time. Now I am ambivalent about attending – I don't know why – and find myself arriving late.

Jessamyn has the gathered group of about a dozen doing exercises in pairs. The pub is full of locals and I make my way to the bar to order a beer and some delicious-looking homemade French fries. I look around, wondering if our group stands out, but no one seems to be noticing us. I look more closely. I can't tell who might be local, or even what local might mean – here for a few weeks? Months? Years? Decades? Groups of visitors like us are the norm. We don't stand out at all.

When I return to our group there is shuffling to fit me into the circle, but I am happy to stand back and listen. I pass the fries around the group and immediately regret the move. Jessamyn is already struggling to keep focus and momentum. She is sharing tips on creating the mild discomfort that makes an audience laugh more easily, but the group is more focused on the cold draughts, the fries, and enjoying one another. We are saturated. We've had an intense couple of weeks together and now is a time for stories of the trip and talk of home. We've shared profound experiences and a kind of intimacy, yet I know little about these people and their lives. I am interested to know more, but what I am really curious about is what they will do with this experience. Word is being passed around that we'll all meet at the local Thai restaurant for dinner. I quietly slip away from the workshop to poke about town until then.

Dinner is long line-ups, so-so food, distracted conversations. There is talk of going to the pub after dinner. I leave and walk up the valley to read and write in my room.

In the morning, I awake to the realization that today is our last day. I gather my leftover science supplies that are not worth carrying home – plastic tubes of various sizes, pipet tips, microscope slides, cover slips, and the glutaraldehyde that I didn't use – and trek down to UNIS. I am hoping to find a biologist to talk with because I want to hear stories of doing science in Longyearbyen. I end up hanging the bag of stuff on a door handle with a note. I wander into town and find others shopping for souvenirs. We end up sitting in a coffee shop, sharing stories and laughing for a couple of hours before hiking back up to the Coal Miners' Cabins to get ready for the evening banquet. It's a funny idea since most of us will be wearing the same things we've been wearing for the past two weeks, although almost everyone has managed to wash a few things in the laundry facilities at the cabins.

We walk to the Huset restaurant, about a kilometre across the valley on a road of gravel and mud. The restaurant is about halfway between Longyearbyen and our cabins, but on the other side of the valley. We walk past sewer pipes, which flow down the valley in a counter current with hot water being pumped up the hill, simultaneously supplying the cabins and the Bar & Grill with hot water while preventing the sewage from freezing – coal is cheap in Longyearbyen. We pause on the bridge over the Longyearbyen River and listen to the roar as it rages in the muddy glory of full flood.

Arriving at the restaurant, we leave our boots at the door. I am taken aback by the elegance and sophistication of the room. Here, in a remote mining town, is a restaurant with the ambiance to rival any fancy big-city restaurant I've ever encountered. The lighting is exquisite, the soundscape pleasing (a gentle hum of conversation over quiet jazz), and behind the polished wood bar, an impressive selection of spirits. I hadn't realized that the Huset is known internationally for its wine collection. We have a section of the restaurant to ourselves and we luxuriate in the comfort of the spacious lounge. After living in close quarters for fifteen days, we are relaxed with one another. There is an abundance of warmth and fondness.

I no longer feel like an outsider. Tonight, I am hugged. I feel understood and appreciated, as I have come to understand and appreciate so many in this group. Change is motivated by connecting on values, not by sharing data. And yet, given that the laws of nature will trump any story we decide to tell ourselves, the science needs to be accessible. I am thanked for giving the climate talk and I am grateful that these artists embraced our discussions of the science. Even the most passionate climate campaigners will be vulnerable to "green washing" without the tools to access and evaluate the data. I feel I have made a contribution.

I buy Benja a beer and invite him to sit with me on a couch off to the side where it is a bit quieter. I ask him to tell me more about the museum that he and his brother are setting up for the children of his village by the sea in Patagonia. He tells me of their renovation of an abandoned (but structurally sound) building. He describes how the two brothers (Benja a science student, his brother an artist) crafted a space well-lit with natural light. Their first specimen, the specimen that launched the idea, was a beached whale whose bones they meticulously cleaned and assembled by hand. The brothers are setting up programs for the local children and recently won a government grant to buy books for a library. They are raising money to build shelves for the books. Benja wants to teach the children about local ecology, about whales and plankton. I ask if they have a microscope. They do not. I think of the collection of microscopes in my lab back home. "Would you like to take the microscope I used on the ship back to Patagonia with you?" A month from now Benja will send me a photo with a small group of children of various ages standing in the museum, behind the microscope set up on a table. They are holding a sign that says, "Thank you."

The banquet dinner is reindeer with lingonberries. It is the perfect send-off meal, although not everyone is comfortable with eating game. We lounge around for a bit after dinner. Some of us wish for music and dancing, but it isn't happening. We bundle up for the walk back to the cabins.

Tomorrow, most of us will begin our journeys to distant homes: Adelaide, Brighton, Regina, Los Angeles, Galway, Rio de Janeiro, Perth, Minneapolis, and Copenhagen, to name a few. Wherever we land, we'll continue to share the thin skin of atmosphere that connects us all. What will we make of this experience? Will we have a net positive impact on the atmosphere? I am left feeling unsettled.

HOME

It's May 2018 and I've been home from the Arctic for almost eleven months. Two days ago, together with students from my lab, I hiked up Hollyburn Mountain to collect snow algae. The snow was dense and we were able to walk on the surface without snowshoes, only occasionally sinking in up to a knee (or a crotch). The weather was a mix of sun and cloud, the temperature perfect for hiking, the cool air scented with fir and spruce, the alpine forest permeated with the soothing sound of low-hooting dusky grouse. This being the so-called "shoulder season" for outdoor enthusiasts, we didn't see any other people – too late for the cross-country ski crowd and too early for the hikers.

We came to a spot where a spruce tree had fallen across the trail. Strutting up and down along the trunk of the fallen tree was a male grouse, proud and determined in his elegant plumage and his bright orange caterpillar eyebrows. Occasionally he would spread his tail in display and puff up the red air sacs under his neck, hooting the low-pitched riff we had been hearing from his brethren at almost every turn in the trail. This guy was hyped up and aggressively territorial. He hopped off the log and swaggered up to me and around me, threatening to peck my leg if we didn't move along. We moved along, hopping over his log and continuing up the hill, but there he was, right at my heels, chasing us! We stopped and I danced a little dance with this grouse, which my student named "Ricky," before continuing on to collect our samples of snow. On the way back down, I was cautiously approaching Ricky's log when he caught me by surprise, flying down from a tree after I had passed, chasing me down the hill, over his log and beyond.

We have been sampling snow from various local mountains for the past three weeks, catching the early stages of the spring bloom and watching the snow turn bronze, green, and various shades of red. One of my graduate students, Casey Engstrom, spent several years as a field biologist before returning to graduate school. He is a naturalist at heart, and it's a special joy to be in the mountains with him.

This morning, when we found a patch of red snow with an unusual tint, Casey dropped to his knees and pulled out his hand lens. With his nose to the snow he described what he was seeing: "The red ones are so big that I can see individual cells! The meltwater is pale green. It must be teeming with those tiny green cells we've seen in the lab." All of this is cool enough, but suddenly Casey lets out a squawk of surprise, "Ah! There is … something big … swimming …! A rotifer …? Yes! A rotifer!" I grin. Casey is seeing one of van Leeuwenhoek's animalcules. Casey gets up and passes me the lens – it's my turn to get down on my belly and peer at these organisms, living out their lives on the snow. "Some of the red cells are growing in clusters. It looks like they are clinging to snow crystals, like lichens growing on rocks." Back in the lab, we photograph the living jewels under the microscope and PhD student Kurt Yakimovich is keen to prepare DNA so we can identify the species by sequence.

It thrills me that Kurt and Casey are experiencing wonder and having their turn at this soul-satisfying work. For a moment I am lost in nostalgia for a time when I found satisfaction in pursuing my curiosity about the workings of life. Now, the wonder is tempered with sorrow and I am driven in a different direction.

I still struggle with conversations about climate change, especially with other scientists. It has been a decade since my trip to Dresden. At a recent departmental retreat at Simon Fraser University, we discussed our seminar program for the coming year – how to attract interesting speakers, those doing leading-edge research in molecular biology and biochemistry, to present a seminar and spend a day or two meeting with small groups of us to talk science. It is how things are done, and I agree that these face-to-face discussions are powerful drivers of creative science. When I raise the issue of the carbon cost of air travel and suggest alternatives, the room is quiet. I would like to see us shift from a financial budget to a carbon budget. I am politely listened to, there are a few murmurs of "Good idea" and "Yes, we should think about that," and then we are on to the next item on the agenda. Have I become the crone who is politely given space to speak, and is then ignored? I feel like screaming, "Wake up!" I think of my great-grandfather stuck in his cabin, "I am near crazy for being such a fool." But then I let it go. I don't choose to fight this battle.

I watch as the whole of Canada is being drawn into a political circus under the Kinder Morgan tent. Three and a half years after I was sued by Kinder Morgan and arrested on Burnaby Mountain, the controversy rages on. The political rhetoric is increasingly bizarre. Prime Minister Justin Trudeau and the minister of the environment and climate change are telling Canadians, "If this pipeline doesn't get built, we can't meet our climate targets." The truth is that we cannot meet climate targets if it does get built. This double-speak is from the government that approved the project after a review they had previously admitted was seriously flawed.

There remains a long list of outstanding conditions, something like one thousand permits yet to be filled, and fifteen outstanding lawsuits against the project. The Government of Alberta responded to BC's opposition with a boycott of BC wine (some of us did our best to help out the growers). In the middle of what some were calling "a constitutional crisis," Kinder Morgan threatened to cancel the project. The Trudeau government announced a deal to purchase the pipeline from Kinder Morgan for $4.5 billion, with billions more from public coffers to follow for construction of the new pipeline. Ay yi yi! So much political energy and taxpayer dollars invested in a fool's project. The battle over this pipeline is far from over – it frustrates and angers me that so many good people are pouring their personal resources, hearts and souls, into a battle that by all rights shouldn't need to be fought. Why would our government be acting contrary to the health of the planet, the rights of Indigenous peoples, a healthy society? Do I have something wrong? What am I missing?

For a long time, I wanted to understand why this was happening. Is the federal government forcing this pipeline on Canada because of a backroom deal with Alberta? Or is it because of the risk of being sued by

Kinder Morgan under Chapter 11 of NAFTA for the loss of future profits if the pipeline isn't built? Or perhaps it is related to Chapter 6 of NAFTA, the proportionality clause that requires us to continue sending oil and gas to the US? Or did we promise China that we would build this pipeline in another "free trade" agreement? Or, perhaps Trudeau backed himself into a political corner and fell for an elegant con by those brilliant ex-Enron executives running Kinder Morgan. This last possibility resonates. Evidence abounds that climate action will require a large economic shift, and, sadly, it is no surprise those continuing to invest in making their fortunes on the status quo economy are lobbying hard to prevent change.

Finally, I let it go. I don't know why our federal government is so adamant about building this pipeline, and the reasons no longer matter to me. What matters is that the public has not been told the truth about their motivations, because what we have been told doesn't make sense; independent investigative journalists, economists, and scientists have repeatedly revealed the fallacies and lies. Trudeau, his cabinet, and the corporate lobbyists and executives that have captured them are one and all on the wrong side of history. Sadly, they are not alone.

I am having trouble sleeping because of a constant drone. I can't tell how much of it is the hum of the surrounding buildings, and how much travels across the water from the generators on a dozen or more giant cargo ships and tankers at anchor in the bay, awaiting their turn at dock, bright lights outshining the suburban neighbourhoods on the peninsula beyond. My mind is trapped by the idea of ships full of junk feeding consumption driven by skilled marketers, shiny plastic in exchange for nature, all to enrich the rich. I can't tell whether the sound of engine noise through the night is getting worse, or I am getting more sensitive. Last week I commented to a friend, "It sounds like those relentless engines in *Metropolis*." He chuckled and reminded me that *Metropolis* was a silent movie. I want to move out of the city. I recognize the option to move as a privilege.

The average life expectancy of a Canadian woman is 82.14 years. That means that as I write this, I can expect to live for another 7,413 days (plus or minus about the same number; it freaks me out a bit how much less it is with each round of editing this book). Life will go on after me as it did before me. In the meantime, this is my time to live. How much of my one precious life will I give to this humanity-defining moment? What really matters?

It's early August, 2018. I've been struggling to wrap up this book. July was hard. Wildfires are burning all around the northern hemisphere, from Greece to above the Arctic Circle in Sweden. There are over five hundred fires burning in British Columbia. For the third summer of the past four, the air here in Coast Salish territory is hot and filled with smoke. The numbers aren't in yet, but July may have been the hottest month on record, not just here, but globally. People have been dying from heat waves, including in Japan and in Montreal. Climate change is announcing itself, and the heat is just one example.

Uncertainty looms. We don't yet know the impacts of continued warming on our local environment and our social structures. It's hard to plan. It's hard to know what to do. There remains a difference between how much worse things will get with business-as-usual versus prompt and serious action, but how much difference? For some, hope lives in that difference, and hope dwindles as delay diminishes our ability to alter the trajectory.

In *Hope in the Dark*, Rebecca Solnit writes, "Despair is often premature: it's a form of impatience, as well as of certainty." Solnit bolsters her case for hope with example after example of stunning social change, often arriving in the dark with a speed and force unforeseen. I think about hydrogen fuel cells, next-generation nuclear, carbon capture, innovations in agriculture and building design, and, perhaps most importantly, degrowth, changing social values, and restored democracies. Climate change is a complex problem – it will take all of these things and more, but also, everything helps. If hope is what you need, it can be found.

I mourn the losses that are inevitable – the magnificent creatures of the Arctic summer sea ice; the loss of old growth forests on Vancouver Island; the suffering and deaths caused by heat waves. Extended droughts and famine. Wildfires, superstorms, and floods. I despair because of powerful political opposition to climate action. My personal struggle is no longer about whether to hope or despair.

Global warming is ongoing, and for many things I love, it is too late for hope. Last night I had a strange dream. A friend I rarely see was in this dream. I think of him as wise, perhaps because from a distance he saw me burning out early in the election campaign, and arranged for me to get out of the city for a break. I don't remember much from this dream, just one short thing – my friend saying to me, "How can you not know? You need to change your thinking. You are the saddest person I know." Strangely, on waking, I believed I knew what he meant.

I thought my job was to take care of myself and recover from burnout so I could once again be my warrior self, defending polar bears, microbes, and the generations of humans that follow, but it isn't as simple as that. In the process of reading my journals and assembling this chronicle, I became aware of my growing irritability, low-grade depression, and sense of separation from others. Burnout to be sure, but also a failure to process grief. How does one mourn something so big and abstract and at the same time profoundly personal: the world my son will inherit, the loss of the rich, old-growth forests of my youth, the loss of summer sea ice? What would healthy grief look like?

Lately, I have found some peace – at least intermittently – and I've noticed a richer quality to life. But I can only do this a little at a time. I am terrified by the thought of opening myself to this grief. I've leaned heavily on an evolutionary perspective, an intellectual grieving that may not adequately release me. I am keen to turn my attention to a painting project because I am curious whether the more visceral experience of that form might take my grief to a new place, but that too, I know, is missing something important.

A young activist friend is one of the happiest people I know. When she was a college student, an accident left her with chronic pain. As a millennial, she became an adult in a world chest-deep in existential angst. Grace Nosek lives and breathes climate justice activism. She also loves to dance and laugh with friends. She gives so much that I'm moved to caution her against burnout. She smiles patiently and wonders if we should order dessert. Grace is engaged in a collaborative network of people co-creating events and projects, from climate solutions to pipeline resistance. The circle is ever-widening as people engage with building the future. Despair lurks, but the community is attentive and caring. Young people like Grace inspire me. They recognize the grief; they work with it and through it; they pull me from my isolation.

There is no denying the darkness of what the cheater class has done to our planet. Acknowledging the constant pain that comes with that knowledge has been part of my healing. Letting go of my investment in particular outcomes has also been important. Whether or not the pipeline gets built no longer feels like life or death, but supporting those on the front lines of activism and politics remains an important part of my local efforts to change how we do things. Today, I see the struggle we are in as the timeless evolutionary struggle for power. Will the cheaters among us be the demise of our species, or will compassion and ecological wisdom prevail? For me, that is the big unknown within which I live.

At the recent wedding of another young friend, Hannah Campbell (the artist who did the Arctic Circle residency a few years ago), there were among the guests many people from the 2014 Burnaby Mountain protests. We reminisced, we laughed, and we danced. I had been feeling dispirited, but on hearing from a few of these young people that my actions had inspired them, and learning of the diverse projects they are now engaged with, it struck me how we're radiating out, building a giant web that is the future, pinching off the lifeblood that feeds builders of pipelines and needless plastic gadgets. How much of a difference will we make? Perhaps, more than we might imagine, yet less than we'd wish. Hope and despair are ephemeral. What matters, is we have found a way to live well, however desperate the reality of our times. We danced in a big circle. Now and then someone danced into the middle and inspired others; the circle fragmented, some clusters danced with abandon, others stopped to talk. And so, I keep on, embracing the responsibility of being human at this singular moment in the history of Earth.

I'm haunted by the vision of the polar bear sitting on the ridge, watching. I feel bad that we interrupted his day because I imagine he was on a quest for his next meal. If the bear was after that bearded seal we saw lounging on an ice floe in the middle of the bay, I doubt he succeeded – there was too much open water. That lone bear, watching us from his post on the ridge, haunts me like all of Nature sitting in judgment, wondering perhaps whether our remorse will drive us to reassess our place in the world.

Acknowledgments

I began writing *Watermelon Snow* on the shared territories of the Squamish, Tsleil-Waututh, and Musqueam First Nations; I completed the work on Snuneymuxw territory. All of these lands are unceded, that is to say, occupied. I acknowledge my responsibility to join in the work of decolonization. Huy ch q'u.

The villanelle that appears on page 54 was previously in the online literary magazine *Numéro Cinq*. An earlier version of the section "On Reasons to Oppose a Pipeline" appeared in the *National Observer*. The poems by Mary Oliver, A.R. Ammons, and Stephen Collis have been used with permission from, respectively, Charlotte Sheedy Literary Agency, Inc., W.W. Norton and Company, and Talonbooks. The maps of the high Arctic and Svalbard were drawn by William L. Nelson. The route of the *Antigua* was plotted by Sarah Gerats.

Many people helped build this book. My deepest bow of gratitude is to Jill Margo, who got me started writing and stayed with me as developmental editor and gentle mentor. Next up are the friends who generously read versions of the manuscript, catching rough spots and helping me see the work in a different light (in order of drafts read from early to late): Grace Nosek, Richard Sheehy, Marjory Lang, David Johnstone, Kathryn Harrison, Andrew Templeton, Stephen Collis, Marina Julian, and Mary Maillard. A special thanks to Keith Maillard and John Pearce, whose comments on the manuscript, together with an introduction by Laura Cameron, led me to just the right acquisitions editor, Mark Abley of MQUP. With grace and skill, Mark guided me through the peer review process and provided numerous insightful suggestions. I also thank three anonymous reviewers and three editors, Carmiel Banasky, Andrew Nosek, and Correy Baldwin, who each in their way improved the quality of the work. Dr Nadine Mengis checked the veracity of my climate science communication (remaining errors are, of course, my own).

I am deeply grateful to Vancouver-based environmental philanthropist Rudy North – former investment manager, lifelong fan of science, and citizen concerned about global warming – who sponsored me on the Arctic

Circle expedition. With great fondness, I thank all of my shipmates on the *Antigua*. I am especially indebted to Sarah Gerats for her leadership and for keeping the log that helped jog my memory when my notes failed.

Finally, I am grateful to all of those in my life – family, friends, students, and colleagues – whose conversations, insights, and kindness inspire and sustain me.

Glossary and Notes

ARCHAEA

Archaea look just like bacteria. There isn't a microscope that would allow you to tell them apart. Yet, differences in their genes tell us they branched away from the bacterial lineage a long time ago. Archaea are found with bacteria living in hot springs, soils, oceans, and in watermelon snow. Over their long independent evolutionary history, archaea made some unique discoveries. For example, only in the archaeal lineage did life hit upon a way to squeak the last drop from the digestion of biomass in the absence of oxygen. They do this by producing methane – a significantly more potent greenhouse gas than carbon dioxide. These are the organisms found deep in the compost pile, in thawing permafrost, and in the guts of ruminants.

BELUGA

Known to American novelist Herman Melville (in his chapter on "Cetology" in *Moby Dick*, 1851) as the "Iceberg Whale," the beluga is about the same size as its only close relative, the narwhal. Both are found only in Arctic and subarctic waters. Beluga whales are highly social and communicate with a sophisticated language of clicks, whistles, and clangs.

BERGY BITS

"Bergy bits" is an official designation for pieces of ice that are smaller than an iceberg but bigger than "growlers." According to NOAA, bergy bits float greater than three feet but less than sixteen feet above the surface of the sea. They can originate from glaciers, shelf ice, or a large iceberg. Growlers are smaller – as the NOAA website says, "roughly the size of a truck or a grand piano." In Svalbard in June, we saw few, if any, bona fide icebergs, but bergy bits and growlers were everywhere. I didn't know the term "growlers," so in this book, both bergy bits and growlers are referred to as bergy bits.

CALVING

To calve, when said of an iceberg or glacier, means to cleave and shed a smaller mass of ice – a bergy bit, for example. In our Svalbard experience, calving is often accompanied by the shedding of masses of smaller bits of ice. Rather than cleaving to form large icebergs, the Svalbard glaciers appear to be crumbling into the ocean. Calving sounds much like a gunshot – so much so that shooting a gun in the air doesn't deter approaching polar bears because they are inured to the sound.

CHLAMYDOMONAS

Chlamydomonas reinhardtii is the species of single-celled green alga I studied for most of my scientific career (see quarmby.ca). For two decades, I attended the biannual international *Chlamydomonas* conference, where a few hundred of us would talk excitedly about green algae for six days straight. Because many people have worked on *Chlamydomonas* for a long time, we know a lot about it. Using this knowledge, we can probe deeply into the fundamentals of how cells work. Many of the discoveries made by the community of *Chlamydomonas* researchers have been highly impactful. For example, in the quest to understand how *Chlamydomonas* senses light, researchers discovered a molecule that became the foundation of optogenetics, a technology that has transformed neuroscience (Hegemann and Nagel 2013).

CHOANOFLAGELLATES

Choanoflagellates are single-celled organisms that live in marine, fresh, and brackish water. At the top of each bulbous cell sits an Elizabethan-style collar, from the centre of which protrudes an elegant, long cilium. This striking morphology is similar to individual cells in sponges (phylum Porifera). Because of this, choanoflagellates have long been considered the closest living relative of animals. Genomic confirmation of that close relationship and numerous other fascinating studies of choanoflagellates have been done in the lab of Nicole King (see kinglab.berkeley.edu).

CILIA

Cilia are tail-like structures that protrude from the surface of cells. Some are small and still, serving as cellular antennae that detect and translate chemical signals from the environment. Others are longer and move in elegant waves, sometimes like a whip, other times like a breaststroke. The whip-like beat of a cilium propels a sperm cell; the breaststroke of two upper cilia pull *Chlamydomonas* cells through water. Some cells that are anchored in tissues, such as those forming the lining of our respiratory tract, have large bundles of cilia that beat in unison, moving mucus-trapped dust up and out, keeping our airways clear of debris. I am fascinated by the mystery of how the molecular motors arrayed along the length and around the circumference of cilia are turned on and off in rolling waves that generate different waveforms and beat frequencies.

DARWIN, CHARLES (1809–1882)

Some North American evolutionary biologists assiduously avoid two words when speaking to the public: "evolution" and "Darwin." Apparently, audiences are open to the content as long as the labels aren't applied. In contrast, readers of *Watermelon Snow* will, I believe, delight in the astute observations of nature to be found in Darwin's original journals. For example, in his book *The Voyage of the Beagle* (first published in 1839), Darwin documents a hike over the Andes from Santiago, Chile. His entry for 20 March 1835 notes an intriguing find near Paso de los Piuquenes:

> On several patches of the snow I found the Protococcus nivalis, or red snow, so well known from the accounts of Arctic navigators. My attention was called to it by observing the footsteps of the mules stained a pale red, as if their hoofs had been slightly bloody. I at first thought that it was owing to dust blown from the surrounding mountains of red porphyry; for from the magnifying power of the crystals of snow, the groups of these microscopical plants appeared like coarse particles. The snow was coloured only where it had thawed very rapidly, or had been accidentally crushed. A little rubbed on paper gave it a faint rose tinge mingled with a little brick-red. I afterwards

scraped some off the paper, and found that it consisted of groups of little spheres in colourless cases, each the thousandth part of an inch in diameter.

E. COLI

Escherichia coli, the infamous gut microbe, variants of which can wreak havoc with human health, grows rapidly and is one of the easiest beasts to study in the lab. It and a few other bacteria serve as models for understanding microbial-based pathogenesis. They also serve as tools for the experimental dissection of fundamental biochemical processes. From these studies we have learned that although bacteria are small, they are, in their way, sophisticated. This should not surprise us. After all, they've been on a path of evolutionary self-improvement as long as we have.

EUKARYOTIC CELLS

All multicellular organisms, from jellyfish to roses and ravens, are built of eukaryotic cells. Relative to prokaryotic cells (bacteria and archaea), eukaryotic cells are huge and filled with complex structures like a nucleus, mitochondria, and, if they are a plant or an alga, chloroplasts. Some eukaryotic cells, like *Chlamydomonas* and choanoflagellates, are free-living as single cells and they, too, are large and complex, often carrying appendages such as cilia.

ICE-FREE ARCTIC OCEAN

When scientists speak about an ice-free Arctic, they are talking about the central ocean and the North Pole. This area will be free of ice well before we lose some of the thicker coastal ice. Note also that the arrival of consistently ice-free summers will follow some years behind the occurrence of the first ice-free summer.

KEELING CURVE

Data on atmospheric carbon dioxide levels are publicly available from the Scripps Institute of Oceanography at the University of California, San Diego. The site provides data up to the current hourly average, past readings, and scenarios for possible future levels. (See scripps.ucsd. edu/programs/keelingcurve).

PROCHLOROCOCCUS

Prochlorococcus are a form of bacteria that discovered how to do photosynthesis. These tiny cells are the direct descendants of the microbes that first poisoned Earth's atmosphere with oxygen (see page 143). They live in all of the world's oceans and produce a large fraction of the oxygen we breathe, yet we didn't even know they existed until Penny Chisholm and her MIT team first reported *Prochlorococcus* in 1988. The Chisholm Lab continues to uncover the fascinating biology and ecological relationships of these important microbes. Together with a co-author, Chisholm has written a series of children's books about *Prochlorococcus* (see chisholmlab.mit.edu).

SYNTHETIC BIOLOGY

The effort to understand how life arose from non-life is a completely different undertaking than synthetic biology, which is sophisticated genetic modification of existing organisms for a panoply of human purposes. Molecular biologists know how to synthesize DNA – even strands long enough to encode an entire (stripped-down) bacterial genome. We also know how to replace the chromosome of a living bacterial cell with an artificial one that will support life. All of this is impressive (and maybe a bit creepy). But it is not even close to creating life from non-life. To begin the process of animating the inanimate would require the discovery of a means to capture and transform energy (see page 137).

TIPPING POINTS, TIPPING CASCADES, AND HOTHOUSE EARTH

A tipping point occurs when a threshold is crossed and feedbacks become self-perpetuating. For example, we face a potential tipping point when permafrost thaws and releases carbon. In this case, there is an amplifying feedback loop – released carbon (in the form of methane and carbon dioxide) warms the atmosphere, causing more thawing, which in turn causes a further release of carbon, and so on. There is a threshold at which the amplifying feedbacks (also known as positive feedbacks) rapidly accelerate until all of the permafrost is melted. As long as these processes are not moving too fast, other Earth systems, including human manipulations of those systems, have the potential to counter the positive feedbacks.

A tipping cascade occurs when one tipped system triggers another. For example, if the melting of the Greenland ice sheet crosses its tipping point, the cold fresh water that flows into the Atlantic will slow the Atlantic meridional ocean circulation. Together, the melted ice sheet and the stalled ocean circulation would cause sea level rise and heat accumulation in the Southern Ocean, which in turn would accelerate the melting of the East Antarctic Ice Sheet. Hothouse Earth would be an inevitable outcome. Steffen and colleagues (2018) write:

> In the dominant climate change narrative, humans are an external force driving change to the Earth System in a largely linear, deterministic way; the higher the forcing in terms of anthropogenic greenhouse gas emissions, the higher the global average temperature. However, our analysis argues that human societies and our activities need to be recast as an integral, interacting component of a complex, adaptive Earth System. This framing puts the focus not only on human system dynamics that reduce greenhouse gas emissions but also, on those that create or enhance negative feedbacks that reduce the risk that the Earth System will cross a planetary threshold and lock into a Hothouse Earth pathway.

In other words, preserving old growth forests is as important as not building new pipelines. It is possible that human activity has already pushed carbon and temperature past thresholds sufficient to initiate a tipping cascade to Hothouse Earth. However, it is also possible that human actions could still pull us back from the brink.

WATERMELON SNOW

One of the first field samples of red snow was collected in Baffin Bay during the 1818 expedition of Captain John Ross (see Leya 2013). The search for a Northwest Passage – a route along the northern coast of America to the Pacific Ocean and the markets of Asia – was, by 1818, known to be so far north that, if it existed at all, it would not provide a reliable trade route (not, that is, until the globe warmed). Like others of its time, the Ross expedition was more in the spirit of exploration – and keeping the British Navy employed after the defeat of Napoleon. In his published account of the journey, tucked between pages 138 and 139, is a foldout engraving of a gorgeous colour drawing by Ross, titled "Crimson Cliffs. A View of the Coloured Snow in Lat. 76. 25N. & Long. 65. W." Ross dispatched a landing party to investigate the cause of the deep crimson colour. Back on the ship, "the snow was immediately examined by a microscope, magnifying 110 times, and the substance appeared to consist of particles like a very minute round seed, which were exactly of the same size, and of a deep red colour: on some of the particles a small dark speck was also seen. It was the general opinion of the officers who examined it by the microscope, that it must be vegetable."

Sources and Further Reading

Ammons, A.R. *The Really Short Poems of A. R. Ammons*. New York: Norton, 1990.

Berton, Pierre. *The Arctic Grail: The Quest for the North West Passage and the North Pole 1818–1909*. Toronto, ON: Anchor, 1988.

Braakman, Rogier, Michael J. Follows, and Sallie W. Chisholm. "Metabolic Evolution and the Self-Organization of Ecosystems." *Proceedings of the National Academy of Sciences of the United States of America* 114 (2017): E3091.

Bringhurst, Robert, and Jan Zwicky. *Learning to Die: Wisdom in the Age of Climate Crisis*. Regina, SK: University of Regina Press, 2018.

Canadian Press. "Indigenous Activist Kanahus Manuel Arrested after Trans Mountain Protest in BC." *National Observer*, 15 July 2018.

Collis, Stephen. *Once in Blockadia*. Vancouver: Talonbooks, 2017.

– *Almost Islands: Phyllis Webb and the Pursuit of the Unwritten*. Vancouver: Talonbooks, 2018.

Cvijanovic, Ivana, Benjamin D. Santer, Céline Bonfils, Donald D. Lucas, John C. H. Chiang, and Susan R. Zimmerman. "Future Loss of Arctic Sea-Ice Cover Could Drive Substantial Decrease in California's Rainfall." *Nature Communications* 8 (2017): 1,947.

Darwin, Charles. *Voyage of the Beagle*. Washington, DC: National Geographic Adventure Classics edition, 2004.

– *The Origin of Species by Means of Natural Selection or the Preservation of Favored Races in the Struggle for Life*. New York: Modern Library, dual bound edition, 1960.

– *The Descent of Man and Selection in Relation to Sex*. New York: Modern Library, dual bound edition, 1960.

Frid, Alejandro. *Changing Tides: An Ecologist's Journey to Make Peace with the Anthropocene*. Gabriola Island, BC: New Society Publishers, 2019.

Gibson, D.G., J.I. Glass, C. Lartigue, V.N. Noskov, R.-Y. Chuang, M.A. Algire, G.A. Benders, M.G. Montague, L. Ma, M.M. Moodie, C. Merryman, S. Vashee, R. Krishnakumar, N. Assad-Garcia, C. Andrews-Pfannkoch, E.A. Denisova, L. Young, Z.-Q. Qi, T.H.

Segall-Shapiro, C.H. Calvey, P.P. Parmar, C.A. Hutchison III, H.O. Smith, and J.C. Venter. "Creation of a Bacterial Cell Controlled by a Chemically Synthesized Genome." *Science* 329 (2010): 52–6.

Goodenough, Ursula. *The Sacred Depths of Nature*. New York: Oxford University Press, 1998.

Hansen, James. "On the Reticence of Scientists," blog post, 2017. See the 26 October 2017 link on Hansen's Columbia University page, http://www.columbia.edu/~jeh1/mailings.

Hansen, J., D. Johnson, A. Lacis, S. Lebedeff, P. Lee, D. Rind, and G. Russell. "Climate Impact of Increasing Atmospheric Carbon Dioxide." *Science* 213 (1981): 957.

Hansen, J., I. Fung, A. Lacis, D. Rind, S. Lebedeff, R. Ruedy, G. Russell, and P. Stone. "Global Climate Changes as Forecast by Goddard Institute for Space Studies Three-Dimensional Model." *Journal of Geophysical Research* 93 (1988): 9,341.

Hansen, J., M. Sato, P. Hearty, R. Ruedy, M. Kelley, V. Masson-Delmotte, G. Russell, G. Tselioudis, J. Cao, E. Rignot, I. Velicogna, B. Tormey, B. Donovan, E. Kandiano, K. von Schuckmann, P. Kharecha, A.N. LeGrande, M. Bauer, and K.-W. Lo. "Ice Melt, Sea Level Rise and Superstorms: Evidence from Paleoclimate Data, Climate Modeling, and Modern Observations That 2°C Global Warming Could Be Dangerous." *Atmospheric Chemistry and Physics* 16 (2016): 3761.

Hansen, J., M. Sato, P. Kharecha, K. von Schuckmann, D.J. Beerling, J. Cao, S. Marcott, V. Masson-Delmotte, M.J. Prather, E.J. Rohling, J. Shakun, P. Smith, A. Lacis, G. Russell, and R. Ruedy. "Young People's Burden: Requirement of Negative CO_2 Emissions." *Earth System Dynamics* 8 (2017): 577.

Hazelbauer, G.L. "Bacterial Chemotaxis: The Early Years of Molecular Studies." *Annual Review of Microbiology* 66 (2012): 285.

Hegemann, Peter, and Georg Nagel. "From Channelrhodopsins to Optogenetics." *EMBO Molecular Medicine* 5 (2013): 173–6.

Huseman, Jennifer, and Damien Short. "'A Slow Industrial Genocide': Tar Sands and the Indigenous Peoples of Northern Alberta." *International Journal of Human Rights* 16 (2012): 216–37.

Jahn, A., J.E. Kay, M.M. Holland, and D.M. Hall. "How Predicatable Is the Timing of a Summer Ice-Free Arctic?" *Geophysical Research*

Letters 43 (2016): 9113. See also guest post by Alexandra Jahn, online at *CarbonBrief*, 25 August 2016.

Jones, Steven J.M., Gregory A. Taylor, Simon Chan, René L. Warren, S. Austin Hammond, Steven Bilobram, Gideon Mordecai, Curtis A. Suttle, Kristina M. Miller, Angela Schulze, Amy M. Chan, Samantha J. Jones, Kane Tse, Irene Li, Dorothy Cheung, Karen L. Mundali, Caleb Choo, Adrian Ally, Noreen Dhalla, Angela K.Y. Tam, Armelle Troussard, Heather Kirk, Pawan Pandoh, Daniel Paulino, Robin J.N. Coope, Andrew J. Nungall, Richard Moore, Yongjun Zhao, Inanc Birol, Yussanne Ma, Marco Marra, and Martin Haulena. "The Genome of the Beluga Whale (*Delphinapterus leucas*)." *Genes* 8, no. 12 (2017): 378.

King, Thomas. *The Truth about Stories: A Native Narrative*. Toronto, ON: Anansi, 2003.

Kolbert, Elizabeth. *The Sixth Extinction: An Unnatural History*. New York: Henry Holt and Company, 2014.

Lane, Nick. *The Vital Question: Energy, Evolution, and the Origins of Complex*. New York: Norton, 2015.

Leya, Thomas. "Snow Algae: Adaptation Strategies to Survive on Snow and Ice." In *Polyextremophiles: Life under Multiple Forms of Stress*, vol. 27, edited by Joseph Seckbach, Aharon Oren, and Helga Stan-Lotter, 401–23. Dordrecht, Netherlands: Springer, 2013.

Lopez, Barry. *Arctic Dreams: Imagination and Desire in a Northern Landscape*. New York: Charles Scribner's Sons, 1986.

McGoogan, Ken. *Dead Reckoning: The Untold Story of the Northwest Passage*. Toronto: HarperCollins, 2007.

Oliver, Mary. *Thirst: Poems by Mary Oliver*. Boston, MA: Beacon Press, 2006.

Pedersen, R.B., H.T. Rapp, H.T. Ingunn, M.D. Lilley, F.J.A.S. Barriga, T. Baumberger, K. Flesland, R. Fonseca, G.L. Früh-Green, and S.L. Jorgensen. "Discovery of a Black Smoker Vent Field and Vent Fauna at That Arctic Mid-Ocean Ridge." *Nature Communications* 1 (2010): 126.

Peet, Fred J. *Miners and Moonshiners: A Personal Account of Adventure and Survival in a Difficult Era*. Victoria, BC: Sono Nis Press, 1983.

Quammen, David. *The Tangled Tree: A Radical New History of Life*. New York: Simon & Schuster, 2018.

Smith, Charlie. "Squamish Nation Calls upon Premier John Horgan to Rethink Approach to Trans Mountain Project in Wake of Court Ruling." *Georgia Straight*, 17 September 2019.

Steffen, W., J. Rockström, K. Richardson, T.M. Lenton, C. Folke, D. Liverman, C.P. Summerhayes, A.D. Barnosky, S.E. Cornell, M. Crucifix, J.F. Donges, I. Fetzer, S.J. Lade, M. Scheffer, R. Winkelmann, and H.J. Schellenhuber. "Trajectories of the Earth System in the Anthropocene." *Proceedings of the National Academy of Sciences of the United States of America* 115 (2018): 8252–9.

Tsleil-Waututh Nation, Treaty, Lands and Resources Department. "Assessment of the TransMountain Pipeline and Tanker Expansion Proposal," North Vancouver, BC, 2012. The full report can be accessed from the Tsleil-Waututh Sacred Trust Website, twnsacredtrust.ca.

Watt, Frederick B. *Great Bear: A Journey Remembered.* Yellowknife, NWT: Outcrop, 1980.

Woese, Carl. R., and Grace E. Fox. "Phylogenetic Structure of the Prokaryotic Domain: The Primary Kingdoms." *Proceedings of the National Academy of Sciences of the United States of America.* 74 (1977): 5088–90.

Woznica, Arielle, Joseph P. Gerdt, Ryan E. Hulett, Jon Clardy, and Nicole King. "Mating in the Closest Living Relatives of Animals Is Induced by a Bacterial Chondroitinase." *Cell* 170 (2017): 1059.

Woznica, Arielle, Christine Beemelmanns, Alexandra M. Cantley, Elizaveta Freinkman, Jon Clardy, and Nicole King. "Bacterial Lipids Activate, Synergize and Inhibit a Developmental Switch in Choanoflagellates." *Proceedings of the National Academy of Sciences of the United States of America.* E113 (2016): 7894.

Wright, Robert. *Nonzero: The Logic of Human Destiny.* New York: Vintage, 2001.

Wright, Robert. *Why Buddhism Is True: The Science and Philosophy of Meditation and Enlightenment.* New York: Simon & Schuster, 2017.

List of Crew and Participants

Crew

Captain: Joachim Schiel
First mate: Paulien Klompmaker
Second mate: Alwin Bootsmann
Deckhand: Ludo Mathijssen
Chef: Sascha Hühn
Service team: Jana Maxová (manager), Alexandra Renes, Sylvi Heerdt
Expedition leader: Sarah Gerats and her dog Nemo
Wilderness guides: Tims Bürgler, Louise Harbo, Benjamin Caceres Murrie

Participants

M. Acuff, J. Anthony Allen, Natalie Arnoldi, Christopher Baker, Carmiel Banasky, Deidre Cavazzi, Rachael Dease, Brett Despotovich, Pablo Serret de Ena, Eric Esterle, Jessamyn Fairfield, Robert Hengeveld, Emma Hoette, Risa Horowitz, Lucy Humphrey, Bruno Keusen, Adam Laity, Hailey Lane, Brandy Leary, Justin Levesque, Cara Levine, Anna McGuffy Clark, Cicilia Östholm, Jesus Mari Perez, Bethan Peters, Beatrice von Preussen, Lynne Quarmby, Cyndi Reeves, Carleen Sheehan, Susan Stewart